MANBOY

by Vince Vawter

Sequel to 'Paperboy' and 'Copyboy'

The 'Boy' Trilogy

WOODLOT PRESS

Louisville, Tennessee

Summary:

Victor Vollmer, introduced to readers in *Paperboy* and *Copyboy*, is 21 years old
now and has been waiting for three years to reunite with Philomene Moreau,
the South Louisiana free spirit who saved him from drowning in the
Mississippi River. Soon after Phil arrives in Memphis, Vic's meticulously
planned weekend comes crashing down as a world event unfolds. Vic, still
dealing with his worrisome stutter, and, Phil, needing badly to share her
secret, grapple with the chaos paralyzing the city. Aiding in their desperate
search to find solace is a wise soul from Vic's past. *Manboy* is a work of
historical fiction set against the actual newspaper headlines of the weekend in
April 1968 that changed the world.

Dedicated to the memory of Nellie Avant.

man • boy (n) A male who, by age, should be a man, but still acts childish, is oblivious of what acting grown-up is about. An insult to point out ridiculous immaturity. A pathetic example of accepting the responsibility of manhood.

–The Urban Dictionary

(Cover illustration – Nellie's House – by CFinleyArt)

Chapter I

April 4, 1968
Thursday

THE GOOD THING about waiting on a train is that you can feel it coming long before you see it.

Nine years ago, when Rat and I were in the seventh grade, we would pedal our coaster-brake bikes to Lenox Station near the Cooper Avenue viaduct and place our palms on the rails. Rat, my best friend back then, said he could tell by the vibrations of the track when the L&N was leaving Union Station in downtown Memphis, seven miles away. Sure enough, a few minutes later we would see it coming down the tracks.

The first few times we waited on the trains we would put quarters on the rails so the train would flatten them. After a while, we decided we were just wasting good quarters. Mature thinking has to begin somewhere.

Rat knew a lot of things back then that I didn't have much of a handle on. Like how to be a good paperboy and how to talk to girls. I wasn't sure if he was ahead of me in such delicate matters or if I was just woefully far behind for my age. I had in mind at some point that I was catching up with him, but I didn't have a way of knowing for sure since Rat and his parents moved out of town and we lost touch.

Rat—his real name was "Art"—but my speech impediment was giving me trouble with the A-sound on the day I first met him, Rat had always been my most reliable measuring stick and was quick to tell me when I was spending too much time thinking about questions that were never meant to be answered.

"You're doing that goofing-off thinking again, Vic," Rat would say. "Lighten up. Take your foot off the brake." I liked the way Rat thought about the world and the incautious way he went about life, but much to my disappointment, I was beginning to understand that I would never be like Rat.

He was all about decisions, and I was all about questions. My over-thinking got the best of me more than I liked to admit, but when I looked back at my friendship with Rat, the troublesome questions that haunted me mostly dealt with matters inconsequential. Deeper queries were coming into my life now that caused visits by my worry-haints. A continual gnawing would grind away inside me when I could least deal with them. My problem was that I felt most vulnerable when I tried to keep the haints at bay, knowing all along they would be waiting to jump on me just around the next corner. I could talk to Rat about most anything, even my stutter that kept me balled-up inside, but he never knew about my worry-haints and how much trouble they caused me.

Rat also was the one who tried to break me of my habit of typing long passages from books. When I found a book or even a magazine with words that felt like they meant something special, I would type a few of the important pages as I read the words in my head.

"Somebody has already typed those words," Rat would yell when he would catch me banging away at my typewriter in my upstairs room. "You're as crazy as a Betsy bug."

"These words are worth typing again," I would counter.

"Once is enough for Pete's sake . . . take your foot off the brake and get on with it," I can hear Rat say. I envied Rat and his no-brakes attitude about life.

Rat had moved away by the time I first found myself out of sorts after typing a long passage from a book. Everybody at school was reading *The Catcher in the Rye*, so I joined them, of course, mainly because the teachers said it was a book we should NOT read because there was a prostitute in it named "Sunny" and a lot of curse words. I became interested in the main character in the story named Holden Caulfield and his mixed-up ways of thinking, so I started in typing passages from the paperback that I held open by placing the top of it under the front lip of my heavy Royal typewriter. I was on page 38 when I came to the sentences where Holden was talking about his brother Allie. I typed:

> *He's dead now. He got leukemia and died when we were up in Maine, on July 18, 1946.*

I typed those sentences, yanked the piece of notebook paper out of the typewriter and stared at it. *July 18, 1946*, is the day I was born. My actual birthday. I couldn't make it work in my head that Allie Caulfield, Holden's brother, died on the day I was born. The date of his death and even the character were fiction, and my birthday was reality. Or was it the other way around? I had to stay away from that book for a couple of weeks and I never dared type from it again because of the way those sentences did me in.

THE CITY OF NEW ORLEANS was due at Central Station at 5:15 p.m. I had been sitting on the wooden-slat bench since 4 o'clock, made more uncomfortable by the wire-bound reporter's notebook I had neglected to take out of my back pocket after my shift at the *Memphis Press-Scimitar* where I worked part-time as a copy clerk. When I started in the summer of 1965, they had called me a "copyboy," but at some point, I discovered that I was listed as "copy clerk" in the company directory.

4

I normally finished my four hours at 8 o'clock in the morning and had planned to go back to campus and take a shower, but on this day the city editor had me work until the middle of the afternoon, typing in names and addresses of hundreds of people arrested during the garbage workers' strike the week before. I needed the extra hours to help me pay for my all-important weekend that I had been looking forward to for months. This was the weekend that was going to be the start of something big for me. I could feel it, and the feeling was just as real as the worry-haints but much more exciting to think about.

It was all I could do not to reach down and test for the slightest vibration in the rails.

Two men in round-top conductor hats, one pushing a railway cart loaded with trunks and suitcases, came down the concrete ramp between the tracks. The oversized iron wheels tapped out a consistent rhythm as the cart rolled over the cracks in the ramp.

I stood.

"How far out?"

It was easier for me to talk while standing because I could shift from one foot to the other in a kind of a dance to help me start my strategically prepared words, a trick I used to help me hide my stutter.

Even though my attempts at spontaneous conversations were getting better now, I still felt the need to map out most of my words ahead of time. Rat never said as much, but lining up and shifting around my words in advance was undoubtedly one of the reasons he thought I kept my foot on the brake too much.

The man walking beside the cart tugged on a silver chain and pulled a pocket watch from his vest.

"Should be just hitting the state line 'bout now," he said, without looking up. "So, another 20 minutes, give or take." I checked my wristwatch. The train, thankfully, was right on time.

If you looked at the railroad tracks straight on, they resembled wavy noodles more than heavy steel rails. How a train ever stayed upright on those spaghetti-like tracks was beyond me, but I didn't have time to worry about railroad engineering or the physics of motion. All I could think about was that Philomene Moreau would soon be getting off that train. I had known her for only four days down in Louisiana and had not seen her in three years, but even with all that separation, she felt like the most important person in my life now.

I COULDN'T WAIT any longer. I stepped off the concrete pad and eased the leather sole of my penny loafer down on the rail nearest to me. The iron rail vibrated with a scant hum that ran straight up through my body. Soon enough a diesel engine with its oscillating single headlight eased around the last curve before it made its straight run into the station. The train's progress was unmercifully slow. I wanted to jump off the loading platform and run toward it but made myself stand in place with my hands stuffed in my pants pockets.

Air brakes hissed. The giant wheels of the City of New Orleans diesel engine whined and then skidded on the rails before coming to a dead stop just a foot from the huge rubber bumper at the end of the track. The railroad conductor who had given me the arrival time placed a stool at the doorway of the lead passenger car. He reached out to assist the first traveler.

Phil ignored the conductor's helping hand, secured her small bag on her shoulder and launched herself out and over the stool, the same way she jumped off her daddy's fishing boat. I realized then that I only had seen her in shorts in our few days together in Louisiana.

Now, she had on a t-shirt loosely tucked into her blue jeans, but not the ragged bell-bottomed kind that the hippie girls on campus wore. Phil's jeans were fresh and rolled up in wide cuffs above her black high-top tennis shoes that she liked to wear on her father's boat.

She looked my way. "Hey, Sporty Boy," she yelled and then waved. "I *garantie* you been right here an hour, sure," she said as she trotted toward me.

Phil had the habit of juicing up her French-Cajun accent when she was excited, bringing out the superfluous "sure" as an exclamation mark to her sentences. We had not seen each other since the few days I had spent with her on my mandated trip to Louisiana in 1965 to try to find the mouth of the Mississippi River. We had been writing each other regularly, but I couldn't tell from her letters if she had changed any of her rambunctious ways that I enjoyed so much. Her acrobatic leap from the train assured me she was the same free spirit that could pilot a small skiff up and down the Mississippi River and dazzle all the old men at a late-night *fais do-do*.

Phil's natural dark curls bounced the same as the day I first met her. Hair styles on girls seemed to be dependent on the trends of the day, but not with Philomene Moreau.

My resolve to stay calm abandoned me. I skipped once and then broke into a run.

Earlier in the day as I was typing in the arrest reports for the newspaper, I had tried to play out in my mind how our greeting at the train station might go after not seeing each other for three years. Would there be a hug? Maybe a peck on the cheek? As usual, Phil was far ahead of me. She wrapped the arm without the shoulder bag around my neck and kissed me. A bona fide lip-lock, as Rat liked to explain to me in detail when he first started going on dates. The three years I had not seen Phil vanished in that moment, and it felt at that instant that she was mine again. Not that she belonged to me—she could never belong to anybody—but that she was physically

in my life once more. She would be with me for a few glorious days
that had begun to feel like they were going to be the start of
something significant in my life.

I had rehearsed how I would ask her about her parents, siblings and
how her classes at the junior college were going. She had written
that the two years of French she was taking almost seemed like
cheating because she was so familiar with that language. She had
also written that she was excited about changing her two-year course
of study from general business classes to emergency medical services.
All those topics that I had practiced in my head for our first meeting
in three years went out the window as soon as soon as she was in my
arms. I should have remembered that my intricate planning and
conversational logistics didn't have much of a chance around Phil.

"I'm as starved as Saint Anthony's mule," she said as we walked off
the loading platform and into the dark, lonely and ornate station
that had seen better days.

"That man on the train tried to charge me three dollars for a
chicken-salad sandwich and a soda. I told him I was more likely to
eat the seat cushions first."

"The Arcade restaurant is across the street," I said. "The food's not
too bad . . . if you like hamburgers and fries."

"Let's get then," she said.

"Have any luggage to collect?"

"You're looking at it," she said, adjusting her shoulder bag. The bag
was the vinyl type you might take to the gym. On the side of the bag
was a helicopter logo. I had invited Phil to my fraternity's big party
of the weekend but didn't mention in my letters that it was the
formal affair of the year. In fact, I had never called it by its name—
the "Old South Ball"—fearing Phil might not be interested in such
formalities. No doubt, Phil would have ignored my classifications

anyway. "Formal" was not a word that carried much weight in Phil's world in the bayou waters of South Louisiana where her ideal day was serving as first mate on her father's charter boat in the Gulf Stream and helping sunburned clients reel in 300-pound yellowfin tunas.

I liked to fool myself into thinking that Phil and I had been equally corresponding with each other during the past three years, but I was the one doing most of the writing. My letters outnumbered hers by at least five to one and sometimes were three or four single-spaced pages to her single hand-written pages. What she didn't know is that I had to slow myself down or the difference would have been closer to ten to one. I asked her once in a letter if all my writing was a bother to her.

"I'm glad you're a rich college boy and can afford all that time and postage," she wrote back, "but keep all those letters coming so I'll know one of those fancy college girls hasn't stuck a gaff hook in you."

While I tried to tell her about all the different things going on at school and my part-time newspaper job, I had not leveled with her about my dire financial circumstances, one of those worry-haints I had talked myself into dealing with by making myself not think about it. My father's significant alimony payments to my mother were stretching his finances thin, and I had explained to him that I didn't need an allowance for college since I had my part-time job. While my intake of funds had been cut drastically, I hadn't thought much about changing my lifestyle, however, and my world had turned into a paycheck-to-paycheck existence, as I barely managed to get by.

On one of the few occasions I was able to call Phil on a free long-distance telephone line at the newspaper, she teased me about some of the more obscure words I had started using in my letters. She called them my "showing-off words."

"Anytime I get a letter, I know I'll have to grab the *dictionnaire*," she said to me on the phone. I told her that we were even because I didn't understand some of her words when she trotted out her French-Cajun *patois*.

"Most boys who turn 21 think it gives them a license to throw down and party," Phil said. "With you, it just means it's time to show off all those big-shot words."

"I like words," I said into the telephone receiver. "Big and small . . . even though I c-c-can't say them r-r-ight."

Phil stopped me with her aggressive shush. I could almost see her hand going up over the telephone line, the same motion with which she gave instructions on her father's charter boat.

"Don't get me going on that, Sporty Boy," she had said.

Three years ago, in our short time together, she had told me I was too self-conscious about my stutter and thought about it more than was good for me. Phil had taken Rat's place as my guide and counselor, encouraging me in her own matter-of-fact way to take my foot off the brake.

I THOUGHT OF MEMPHIS as my city, but Phil led the way across the wide lanes of South Main Street. I was content to follow, if only to be able to look without interruption at her natural mane of unattended curls. She once likened her hair to the scouring pads her mother used to clean pots. I wrote her that her hair reminded me of the pictures I had seen in the school library of the sculpted Venus de Milo, but I had the good sense not to send her that letter.

I thought her transition to college life might have taken her out of the harsh weather elements of South Louisiana, but her dark complexion was not simply the work of the sun. She remained a glorious dark bronze the year around with the same toned body of a worker on the docks.

We picked a window booth just inside the front door of the restaurant. The Arcade was busy at lunch but didn't have much of a crowd late in the day.

"This is where they fixed fried peanut butter and b-b-banana sandwiches for Elvis," I said, pointing to the "Elvis Special" on the menu. I thought about leaving out the word "banana" because it started with a plosive letter, but I wanted to say it for Phil even though I knew I would stutter on it.

"I'll pass on that," Phil said. She ordered a cheeseburger and fries. I told Phil I wasn't hungry because I had a big lunch, but the truth was that seeing her had me too excited to think about putting anything on my stomach.

"Black as the bottom of a well," Phil said, when the waitress asked how she wanted her coffee. While I always used as few words as possible and tried to nip and tuck them as best I could, Phil splattered hers generously on her large canvas for everybody to see.

I didn't interrupt as she filled me in on the goings-on in her hometown of Venice, Louisiana. Certainly, I wanted to see Phil and have her close to me, but what I had quietly longed for in my lonely hours was to hear her unique way of talking. Phil's seamless blend of Cajun-French and English intoxicated me. Common words and phrases took on a new life. I told her in one of our infrequent phone calls that I was trying to learn how to make my writing as interesting as the way she talked. "No secret, Sporty Boy. Just get on with the gettin' on," she had said. I understood. Keep my foot off the brake, but I was finding that to be easier said than done.

In the summer before my college sophomore year, I told Phil in a letter that I was excited about the French class I had signed up for. I didn't tell her the rest of the story—that I had dropped the class after the teacher suggested I take up another foreign language that didn't have so many complex vocalizations demanded by circumflexes, tremas and liaisons. I switched to a political science course with a professor who rarely looked up from his index cards, but at least I had a chance to pass his course.

As Phil ate her cheeseburger, I quizzed her about her family and how they were rebuilding their house that had been devastated by Hurricane Betsy in 1965.

"We 'bout to heal up and harrow over," she said. "When there's not that much to start with, there's not much that needs putting back."

Phil dispatched each of my questions quickly. I recalled that she had been reluctant in Louisiana to talk about her personal life for any length of time. Sprinkling more Tabasco sauce on the last of her fries, she turned the questions back on me.

"Tell me what's going on at your big city newspaper," she said.

The reporter's notebook jabbing my backside gave me an idea. I flipped it open and read from it in the best authoritative radio voice I could muster. When I took on someone else's voice, my stutter was more apt to recede.

"Middling spot cotton closed today on the Memphis Exchange at 25.50 compared with the same 25.50 on Wednesday and 22.25 for the corresponding date last year."

Phil laughed. "So, what does all that gobbledygook mean, Mr. Big Shot Newspaper Reporter?"

"I don't have a clue," I said. "But that's the paragraph I wrote today and the same one that another copy clerk will get the new numbers on and write tomorrow . . . b-b-because . . . I'm taking all of Friday and Saturday off . . . for our b-b-big weekend together."

The staccato excitement in my voice did not translate into an equal enthusiasm in Phil's eyes like I had anticipated. Her downward look did not acknowledge my elation of the days that were ahead of us. Sometimes I let others tell me when to hit the brakes. Phil pushed her plate away that had a few fries left.

"And how 'bout those fancy college classes of yours. You don't talk much about school in your letters, only the people at the newspaper and how much you like working there."

I had not thought much about me not mentioning my schoolwork but, as usual, Phil was correct. I enjoyed my time at the newspaper more than time spent in classrooms. Although my job as a copy clerk was part-time, the newspaper was where I was most comfortable; the place I felt I was learning important things that I needed to know. College classes seemed more like batting practice while working in the newsroom, even as a lowly copy clerk, made me feel like I was in a real ball game.

"Classes are going okay," I said. "But I'm thinking about taking off a year . . . if I can get a reporting internship. A p-p-paid one."

My words surprised me more than they seemed to surprise Phil. I had talked to no one about taking a year off from school and didn't let myself even think about it all the way through. Phil did that to me. Words and thoughts tumbled out of my mouth when I was with her, almost against my will, leaving me no time to pump the brakes.

"Look at you," she said. "Always pestering me like my daddy about staying in school and the value of a good education and all that *busyness,* and now here you go talking about laying out of school for a year."

I didn't have a response, but she gingerly let me off the hook.

"I'm sorry I didn't get you anything for your birthday and I feel bad about not being able to get off work to come to your party," Phil said. I wasn't much on birthday parties, but I was looking forward to turning 21 because somehow it felt closer to Phil's age of 24.

"I'm just glad you're here now . . . and that we have a long weekend to ourselves . . . or mostly to ourselves," I said.

I had told all the fraternity brothers about my special date coming up from Louisiana for our big party, but now I was feeling that I wanted to have her all to myself. No sharing of "my girl" with the brothers. *My Girl* was a popular song that played over and over on the stereo at the fraternity house. The brothers would scream the lyrics—sunshine on a cloudy day, and all that—but the song made me long for Phil so intensely that I would have to leave the room. She wasn't a *girl* anyway, I told myself. She was a *woman* in every sense I could make of the word.

Phil slid her plate to the side and reached across the table to put her hand on top of mine.

"I'm glad to be here, too," she said. "I've been missing you, sure. We spent those three days together running from Hurricane Betsy and then three years apart. All your letters are nice, but I needed to see me some of that real Sporty Boy."

She slapped the top of my hand.

 "Saints alive. I guess I'll need to stop calling you 'Sporty Boy' in front of all your fancy fraternity friends. Do they call you 'Vic' or 'Victor'?"

"Vic," I said. The "V" sound had come out for Phil without the slightest hesitation, prolongation or repetition. Not the slightest hint of a stutter. This was going to be a good weekend.

DESPITE HER RELUCTANCE to talk about her personal life, Phil efficiently answered my questions about her family and about her father's charter fishing operation that he had been rebuilding since the hurricane. I couldn't decide whether to watch her dark eyes, the curls of her hair or how her unpainted lips moved with her treasury of exotic words.

Outside the restaurant, a string of police cars and fire trucks with sirens wailing sped both directions on South Main Street, unusual for downtown Memphis. The clock on the restaurant's wall said it was a little after 6. The rush-hour should have been over.

"This 'bout as noisy here as New Orleans at Mardi Gras," Phil said, as she looked out the window to the street. "Is there always this much commotion around here?"

I shook my head and was lining up the words to tell her about the law against honking your car horn in Memphis that my newspaper had editorialized for, but then I saw a man run out of the train station with panicked strides like he was being chased. He dodged cars, wildly waving his hands as he crossed the wide street and banged open the restaurant's heavy glass door.

"Turn on the radio," he breathlessly yelled to the manager who was counting bills at the cash register. "That guy . . . that Martin Luther King guy . . . has been shot . . . at the Lorraine."

I stared at Phil with a blank look. I instantly felt the long weekend I had joyously anticipated about to be swept away in something that was out of my control, the same way I had looked at Phil three years earlier when the current was taking me out to the Gulf of Mexico on my ill-planned quest initiated by Mr. Spiro to find the mouth of the Mississippi River

Philomene Moreau had been my salvation in the swirling river. All I wanted from her this weekend was some proof that she was the girlfriend that I longed for her to be—*my girl*—but I sensed my few precious days with her were about to be put in jeopardy by circumstances beyond my control. Another swirling river. My foot was pushing down hard on the brake.

"M-m-maybe . . . maybe . . . I n-n-need to get to the new-new-newspaper . . . to see if I can . . . you know . . . help out . . . s-s-s-some."

I wondered when my first jagged stutter of the weekend would show its ugly head to Phil. I had worked hard to put my recalcitrant speech into the background, even though I knew that Phil didn't hold my stutter against me. She had casually let me know in Louisiana that I "sputtered" more than I stuttered, but I was glad to get the first herky-jerky stuttered sentence out of the way on something that wasn't the small talk that both of us had agreed that we never wanted to have anything to do with.

Chapter 2

AS SMALL as Phil's shoulder bag was, it filled up almost half the trunk of my little sports car parked in the train station's lot. When I first met Phil, I had referred to the trunk of my car as the "boot," its British name that I had learned from the owner's manual. She laughed and was quick to let me know that I needed to call it a "trunk" in Louisiana, or I might get a sharp-toed *botte* somewhere I didn't want.

Phil never carried a purse, content to wrap her driver's license inside a few paper bills stuffed in the right back pocket of her jeans.

"I see you still got your same little doodlebug," Phil said, as she slid into the passenger seat. "Didn't we have some kind of *voyage* in this thing with Betsy on our tail, sure?"

Hurricane Betsy had ravaged the Louisiana Coast in 1965, the country's first storm to cause more than a billion dollars in damage. After Phil rescued me from my fall from her boat into the Mississippi River and after she had patched up the gash on my head, we had managed to stay just ahead of the wind and the fury of the hurricane that roared up through the river delta. We had just met, but our frantic escape together from the storm had somehow bound us together in special ways, at least in my mind. And I hoped in hers.

"Only thing missing in this doodle is that old typewriter you hauled around everywhere," she said. "You still got that thing that was near 'bout heavy as an anchor?"

I shook my head in regret. I had intended to send her the short story I had written about having to swap the typewriter for gas money to get back to Memphis after the hurricane, but I couldn't make the writing mean anything beyond the words on the paper, so I tore up the six pages I typed on one of the typewriters at the newspaper.

I took a deep breath. My mind was hopping around like one of Phil's South Louisiana swamp rabbits, trying to come up with a new plan for my much-anticipated weekend that I could feel coming apart with the news that Dr. Martin Luther King had been shot. Even though I was a lowly copy clerk, I knew enough to anticipate the story was big news and that I should check in with the newsroom on the chance I might be needed. Phil, as usual, was taking everything in stride in an outward calmness that I suspected was cover for her own quiet deliberations.

"The Southwestern campus is about 15 m-m-minutes from here," I said. "I can take you to the girls' dorm where you're registered for the weekend, and then I can circle b-b-back to the newspaper to see if they need me. That will give you time to settle in and see how you like the place you're going to be staying . . . when you're not with me. It will give you a chance to get the lay of the land."

I was proud of the details of my plan. "Lay of the land" was one of Phil's phrases that I had picked up down in Louisiana and liked. Words that started with an "l" were my bread and butter.

"Too much running against the current," Phil said. "If the newspaper office is on the way, I'll go with you there. What all you think they'll have you doing, anyhow?"

I didn't know for sure, but I had been working at The *Press-Scimitar* long enough to know that this was an all-hands-on-deck situation. That I would be expected to check in. I had seen how the newsroom could gear up rapidly when a story broke that was considered major, and this was as big as they came in my limited experience.

18

"The AP and UPI wires will be going full b-b-blast and will need extra sorting," I said. "I may n-n-need to pick up film from the photographers and run it back for p-p-processing. I don't know. I've never been involved in something as b-b-big as this."

"You mean that almost floating away to the Gulf of Mexico with your head bashed in and then us outrunning the hurricane all night and day wasn't big enough for you?"

Phil had a point.

"That was b-b-big for me, all right," I said, "but this is a big story for everybody. The p-p-people in the newsroom will be going a mile a minute." I stuttered on the first b-word but not the second. That happened often.

The AM radio in my car had shorted out several months before because my convertible top had started leaking badly. I didn't know any of the circumstances of Dr. King's shooting but could tell in the short drive from the train station to the newspaper offices on Union Avenue that the city was bubbling over with sirens and speeding police cars in what should have been a lazy time at 6:30 on a spring evening, a solid hour past the usual downtown rush hour. The Lorraine Motel, where the man at the restaurant said that Dr. King had been shot, was on Mulberry, a few blocks from the newspaper. I had seen the non-descript motel many times on my copy-clerk runs.

"What was Martin Luther King doing in Memphis anyway?" Phil asked.

"He came to support the garbage workers who are on strike in the city," I said. "He was here about a week ago and came b-b-back yesterday, but I didn't know he was staying at a place so close to the newspaper. The Lorraine is in kind of a rundown area."

"Hard to believe that a man who preaches non-violence the way he does gets shot by somebody," Phil said. "Hope it's not too bad."

I had never known Phil to be a big newspaper reader, but it seemed she could converse with anybody on current events. Even though I pulled dozens of wire stories on the Vietnam War every day, I could tell from her letters that she knew as much as I did about what was happening on the other side of the world. She wrote to me that she could understand why young people were protesting the war. She had asked me in a letter in her no-punches-pulled way if I was going to college to avoid the draft. I wrote her back that I received a 4-F deferment because I was missing half my right knee from a football injury in high school. That was only half the truth. The doctors had also checked off "speech disability" on my processing form after my day-long draft physical. When the doctors gave me the deferment, I was outwardly relieved and privately upset about my inadequacy for service.

Phil continued to ask more questions about the strike, and I told her that Dr. King had planned to lead a protest march on Friday through the streets of Memphis, but the mayor and the city had gone to court to try to get the march stopped.

"He gave a speech last night at a church that made all the n-n-national wires this morning," I said. "Something about how he had been to the mountaintop and had seen the p-p-romised land."

I had read portions of the long speech on the wires that morning and was impressed that the civil rights leader seemed to care for the words he spoke as much as I cared for my words on paper. I found myself typing the words in my head as I read them amid the clackety-clack of the wire machines. The entirety of the speech was transcribed on both the United Press International and the Associated Press wires. I knew the editors would need only one copy of the speech if they decided to use it, so I rolled up the UPI copy, put a rubber band around it and tucked it away in a safe place in my drawer at the copy clerks' table.

THE AREA where I usually parked in the Memphis Publishing Company employee parking lot was full. The *Press-Scimitar* was an afternoon newspaper, and I mainly worked the 4 a.m. shift due to my college class schedule. The morning newspaper would be at full staff and would get the all-important first news break on the story. Circulation trucks were already lining up at the loading dock. The newspaper plant, the one I had worked at part-time for more than three years, felt new and strange at this time of the early evening.

"I guess m-m-maybe you can stay in the car while I run up and see what's going on," I said, switching off the ignition. Phil already had her door open and was stepping out.

"Not to my mind, Vic," Phil said. "I've never been in a newspaper office, and this seems like as good a time as any to check it out."

"But, I don't . . . ." Phil put her hand up, palm facing me, much like she gave orders on her father's charter boat.

"I won't be a bother to you," she said. "I'll just sit in the corner and bide my time. Let's get. Where's the front door?"

I should have known better than to ask Phil to stay in the car. At one time I had even thought about taking her to see where I worked sometime during the weekend, but I had decided against it when I knew I would have to introduce her to people at the newspaper. Even though I was finding new ways to work around my stutter, one of the most difficult things to do was making introductions. So much information had to be exchanged quickly and in the proper sequence. Timing was everything. This rapid exchange that needed to be exact was much the same reason I had never tried to tell jokes. If I had a speech block during the punchline, the joke didn't make any sense and fell flat. If I blocked on my words during an introduction, the hesitation sounded like I had forgotten everybody's name and it made all those around me nervous and look away from me.

I pointed to the two-story opening in the building behind the guard shack. There was no actual door to the five-story plant because the area where employees entered was never closed. The wooden guard shack was a remnant of two years back when there was a union strike at the newspapers. Now, the shack was used for circulation storage. Phil headed off for the entrance and I followed.

Inside the building we passed near several pressmen in their ink-stained uniforms crowded around a transistor radio hung on a nail outside the entrance to the employee shower room. Normally, the radio was used only to listen to Memphis State football and basketball games.

"Okay . . . that's it, men," said the heavy-set man I recognized as the night-side press foreman. He switched off the radio. "They just pronounced him dead at St. Joe Hospital. Get ready, guys. They'll have us printing a bunch of extras tonight."

We took the elevator to the fifth floor of the building that had been converted from its original use as a Ford Motor Company plant. The elevator opened into a dark hall that led to the cavernous newsroom with 20-foot-high ceilings. At this time of day, the room would have been mostly empty except for a night city editor and a reporter or two finishing up stories for the next day, but I saw a dozen people standing in the glass-walled office that belonged to the managing editor, the man who ran the newsroom.

The noises in the room came from the half-dozen Teletype machines spewing out wire copy and the police scanner on the city desk that had been turned up to full volume. The only sounds missing were the staccato clacking of typewriters and the pneumatic tubes spitting out rolled-up galley proofs from the composing room.

The managing editor sat on the edge of his desk with his suit coat on and no necktie. I had never seen him in the office without a thin tie cinched up tight around the collar of his white shirt. He went home around 5 o'clock so he evidently had come back in. The city editor, saw me and motioned for me to join the meeting.

"Tell me where to dock myself," Phil said to me. "You go on and do what you need to do."

I took her over to what qualified as "my desk," the wide tables in the middle of the room where the copy clerks worked. I found her the Final edition of the day's paper. The play headline was the standard fare out of Vietnam about a vague peace initiative, but underneath was the main local story of the day.

10 Dead, 53 Injured in Mid-South Tornadoes

When I wasn't typing in arrest records, I had spent that morning pulling and sorting the Tennessee, Arkansas and Mississippi state wires that made up the story that was put together by the editors on the city desk. The closest tornado to Memphis was in Millington, a northern suburb. Tornadoes rarely made their way into Memphis proper because of its position high on a bluff of the Mississippi River, but my newsroom intuition, meager and untried as it was, told me that another type of fury was about to be unleashed on the city.

"Night side should be ready to handoff to the day desk at four in the morning," the managing editor said to the assembled group. The leader of the newsroom usually talked fast, but the words were coming out in long strings without any breaths. "I just notified the pressroom that we're taking up the paper by four pages tomorrow . . . so we will need lots of copy and art. It's too late for the morning newspaper to add pages because the press is already webbed . . . so we're catching a break there, even though they will get the first story."

"I hope I don't have to tell everybody to look for second-day leads," the managing editor said. "I want somebody monitoring the police scanner twenty-four hours. If I'm not here, call me at home if they catch the shooter no matter what time it is."

He paused. "Better yet, I'll take our two-way radio and keep it with me."

The managing editor continued to look at a list he had scribbled on a yellow pad of paper.

"The morning paper will try to hold as long as they can to see if the shooter is caught, but they can't afford to be late for the Mississippi edition. Let's just hope they catch the shooter on our time."

The newsroom bosses never called the other newspaper by its name even though it was produced in the same building and on the same press. The morning newspaper, while published in Memphis, had the largest circulation of any newspaper in Mississippi. The managing editor told the city desk editors to prepare a story budget and to try and reach all the reporters with their next-day assignments.

"Vic, glad you came back in," the managing editor said when he saw me standing in the back of the group. "We're going to have photogs at the airport, the federal building and two in radio cars. We have called another clerk in to rip copy so you can be available to run film back for processing. Can you work extra tomorrow?"

I nodded.

My carefully crafted plans to spend Friday with Phil were in shambles. Strolls around my college's impressive campus. A walk along the bluffs of the riverfront. Maybe even a trip to see the house where I grew up in midtown. A Friday night party at the fraternity house in advance of the Old South Ball at the Claridge Hotel on Saturday. I had told the fraternity brothers about Phil and was anxious for them to meet her. I hoped the police could catch the assassin soon so some of my special weekend had a chance of being salvaged.

I glanced over at Phil. She had gotten up from the table and was looking at the copy coming off the long bank of newswire machines.

"Okay," the managing editor said. "I'm going home for a few hours, but I'll be back early. Is everybody clear on what we're doing? Remember, I have the extra two-way radio."

The group began to break up. Wayne Chrisman, the reporter who covered the county commission, saw me.

"I thought you told me you were off the clock and didn't have time to change my ribbon," he said. The fast-talking reporter was continually pestering me about his typewriter that he refused to take care of.

"I'm supposed to be off," I said. "I came b-b-back in."

"Who's our visitor?" He nodded towards Phil. I had seen him looking at her in a way I didn't like when I was finding Phil a seat.

"A friend of m-m-mine from Louisiana," I said.

"Isn't she a little bit out of your league?"

I thought of many answers to his condescending question, but I boiled it down to one word that I didn't have any trouble saying.

"No."

"Let's meet her," Wayne said. "Any friend of yours is . . . you know."

Wayne, who never took off his wrinkled suit coat and tie even in the heat of summer, was going to law school at night at Memphis State, studying for his degree so he could take the bar exam. He bragged to me once that he only slept four hours a night and that was all anybody needed who wanted to get ahead. He looked like he mostly slept in his suit. I knew he kept a bottle of pills in the pocket of his coat that had a lot to do with him not needing much sleep. Phil saw us coming over and walked to meet us.

"Wayne, this is Phil from Louisiana."

Two strategic pluses in my favor. "W" was my best starter sound because it came with its own air, and I conveniently skipped the troublesome V-sound in "Venice," the town that Phil was from.

"Phil?" Wayne asked. "You don't look like any 'Phil' I've ever seen."

"Philomene to you then, city boy," she said, with her correcting smile. What Wayne didn't understand is that Phil was out of his league as well.

"Nice," Wayne said. "Welcome to Memphis . . . on this less than auspicious day."

"Good to be here, sure," Phil said. "Looks like I might get to see more of the newspaper than I had planned."

My instincts told me to get back to the car as quickly as possible so I could focus on trying to re-arrange the weekend that was going down the drain in a hurry.

"We need to go," I said. I started to take Phil by the arm but thought better of it. Phil was not a person who led easily.

26

THE TORNADIC WINDS that had come through Memphis earlier in the day left fresher and cooler air in their wake. April had started off humid, but at least the weather was on my side with the pleasant temperatures. If this were the normal day like I had planned, I would be taking Phil to watch the sunset and enjoying the fresh breeze coming over from the Arkansas side of the river.

"Want me to put the top down?" I asked. The girls who had ridden in my car didn't like the convertible because it messed up their hairdos. Phil never paid any attention to her hair.

"Might as well," she said. "Flappy thing is getting so many holes in it, it's not much of a top anyway, is it?"

I explained to Phil how lucky it was that I didn't have to be at work until 8 o'clock the next morning and that she would enjoy getting to meet some of the girls in the dorm at Southwestern where I had arranged for her to stay. My weak explanation was not convincing and, once again, Phil was ahead of me.

"I didn't come up here to play pretty with a bunch of college girls," she said. "So, I'll be going to work with you tomorrow."

My visitor from South Louisiana was not going to make my emergency planning for the weekend easy. It would be nice to have her with me if I was to run film from photographers to the newspaper, but the big obstacle was the company car I would be in. Several years back one of the photographers had a wreck that injured someone in a staff car who was not an employee. There was a lawsuit and company lawyers swooped in and made everyone sign a form stating that any employee would be terminated if a non-employee was given permission to ride in a company car. I thought about using my own car and gas, but I wouldn't have the use of the two-way radio in the staff car to stay in communication with the city desk.

"Let's think about that," I said. "First thing is to get you situated in your dorm and then we can come up with a p-p-plan." I was putting off an inevitable confrontation with Phil, but then she added to her cross-examination.

"I still don't understand why I can't stay in your room at the fraternity house," she said. "It's all yours, right? We can slip in and out, *secrètement*. Nobody needs to be the wiser."

Fraternity houses at Southwestern were designed without living quarters as a matter of school policy, but I was given special permission to stay in a small attic room at the house for one semester because all the dorms were full. My parents had separated, then divorced and both moved away from Memphis, so I couldn't live at home anymore. That was three semesters ago and when I found that no one at the college was keeping track of my living arrangements, I just stayed in the room in the attic of the fraternity house. I paid an extra ten dollars a month in fraternity dues for the tiny space that consisted of little more than a twin-bed mattress on the floor and a reading light. Not even a desk. The bathroom was downstairs with only a sink and toilet. I showered in the school gym and studied in the library. If I had a paper due for class, I used one of the typewriters in the newsroom. A window fan that I bought at a pawn shop for five dollars kept the tiny upstairs room in the fraternity house just bearable in hot weather.

"You'll like the dorm," I said. "It's one of the newer ones on campus and there's even a girl on your floor from N-N-New Orleans. I have a n-n-otion you'll like her." N-words had been good for me lately, but everything seemed to be changing on me.

Phil's silence was uncomfortable as we drove toward campus. Although it was difficult to carry on a conversation in my car with the top down, Phil made sure I knew that she was not thrilled with my plans.

I had not told her that the reason my car was in such bad repair and the reason I had such a ridiculous living arrangement was that my father had to cut the generous allowance he had been giving me. I couldn't afford to get my car fixed or live in a dorm. My father was ordered by the court to pay the hefty college tuition, but not the room and board. He had sold his share of a large Memphis accounting firm and was basically starting over in New Orleans. I had begun working at the *Press-Scimitar* the summer I graduated from high school because I liked it and felt comfortable there. My meager paychecks that I would stuff in my glove box and not cash for several weeks were lifesavers now. I cashed them as soon as I got them each week. I had volunteered to work several hours of overtime to pay for Phil's round-trip train ticket. When I first met Phil, money was not a worry for me. Now, I was broke. Broke as a dog's hind leg, as my old friend Rat liked to say.

THE GUARD STATION at the entrance to the Southwestern campus was never manned at night, so it was a surprise to see a light on inside. A middle-aged uniformed guard, not the older and friendly guy from campus security, stepped out of the pink sandstone hut as my car came to a stop.

"Campus is closed," the guard said emphatically. I noticed he was wearing a holstered pistol. The regular campus security didn't have guns.

"I'm a student," I said, pointing to my campus parking sticker. I wanted to get out of the car and stand, but I kept my seat.

"Then I need to see your student ID and a driver's license." The guard took a flashlight from his back pocket.

"I have my license," I said. "But I guess my s-s-student ID is in my room." I had not seen the plastic ID since I was a freshman.

The guard shined his flashlight in Phil's face.

"I need to see your ID too, ma'am," he said.

"I'm not a student here . . . and glad I'm not," Phil said, glaring at the guard. She was not done with him. "What kind of college you running here anyway? Seems more like a prison to me."

The guard shined his flashlight on my driver's license and then snapped the light back in my face. I got out of the car.

"Look, mister. My girlfriend is registered at Voorhies Hall as a guest for the weekend and I live on campus. What's the b-b-big deal. I've never been stopped like this."

My minor victory of not stuttering on the "V' sound and summoning the nerve to call Phil my "girlfriend" was lost in the guard's next words.

"The 'big deal,' young man, is that I have my orders to shut down this campus to all but registered students," the guard said. "A city curfew is in effect. Students are to remain in their dorms."

I couldn't think of anything to say, so the security guard continued. "A Tennessee National Guard unit is scheduled to arrive on campus early tomorrow."

"National Guard?" I looked at Phil and then back to the guard. "Some of them were just here last week for the pr-pr-protests, but I thought they were all gone."

"They're coming back . . . and a lot more of 'em," the guard said. "Look son, I have a number I can call if you'll let me see your license again, and I'll need your friend's driver's license also."

Phil opened the passenger door and stepped out with one foot, facing me and the guard.

"Vic, turn this doodle around from here," she said. "I didn't want to stay in these girlie dorms here anyway. Let's get."

The guard looked at us and shrugged. "Suit yourself," he said.

I didn't have an alternate plan. I stepped back in the car, put it in reverse and backed out of the gate area. Through the rearview mirror, I saw the guard looking at us with his hands on his hips.

The sun had set, so we couldn't go to the river that I had been intent on showing Phil. I had written to her how the high bluffs were much different in Memphis from the low-slung riverbanks of the Mississippi that she was accustomed to in Louisiana.

My mind was stumbling all over itself for a plan. I had to make a decision on which way to turn on East Parkway. The only thing my scrambled thinking could come up with was to find a place to sit and take stock of the situation in hopes that something more concrete could be decided.

The best coffee shop I knew of in Memphis was the Toddle House near the hospitals on Union Avenue. The restaurant chain, open twenty-four hours a day and seven days a week, had become a Memphis institution. My normal stop there was on the way to the work in the early morning hours.

I was glad to see the lights on in the coffee shop when I pulled into the parking lot that was occupied by only one other car. I didn't recognize the lone waitress in the standard light-green uniform with a small hat pinned to her hair.

"Sit anywhere you like," the waitress said. "I sent everybody else home, but I reckon we're still open for now."

Phil and I sat across from each other in a booth near the cash register.

I had not eaten since a few saltine crackers at mid-morning that I had stashed at the newspaper. An order of hash browns and coffee helped me to focus. I explained to Phil as calmly as I could that I was running a little low on cash and didn't have enough money to check her into a hotel room.

"I'll come up with something," I said. "You took care of me in Louisiana, and I'll take care of you here . . . in my city." Even though I was able to hold off a stutter, my words didn't warrant much confidence.

Phil sipped her coffee without offering rebuttal. I sensed that she was doing what she did best—taking charge by conjuring up plans of her own.

An unmarked police car, a gray Plymouth with black-wall tires and small hubcaps, pulled into the coffee shop's parking lot. The driver parked by the front door in a space that wasn't striped off for parking, almost blocking the entrance. Two men exited the car. The driver left his door open. I recognized the detectives from my copy clerk runs to the police station. Both wore cheap sport coats over their short-sleeve shirts. The coat was to hide the small .38 pistols in holsters on their belts, a policy for detectives, according to one of our cop-shop reporters. One detective, carrying a walkie-talkie radio the size of a first-baseman's mitt, propped the coffee shop door open with a nearby gumball machine.

The waitress already had their coffee poured by the time the detectives took their seats on stools at the counter.

"I thought y'all worked day shifts," the waitress said to the two police officers. "I guess everybody's gettin' called in with all that's going on."

"Might be 'round the clock until the dust settles," the detective with the walkie-talkie said.

My sophomore psychology class had studied "compensatory skills," where the hearing- and sight-impaired developed special abilities to compensate for their specific impairment. I thought I was onto something when I got it into my head that I could eavesdrop on conversations better than most people because of my speech impediment. At any rate, my hearing was excellent, and I found myself listening in on conversations no matter who was having them.

The waitress put the coffee pot back on a burner and leaned both hands on the counter in front of her customers who sat on swivel stools. "So, what's the latest?" she asked. The detectives took turns answering.

"The natives are restless for damn sure," said the older detective. "Fire bombings going on all over town. Windows broken at businesses here and there. Mayor Loeb has imposed a curfew on the city."

"Police chopper was shot at. Had to land on the street but weren't nobody hurt," said the other detective as he poured sugar from a glass container into his coffee. "We're headed north of the city to relieve on a roadblock at 9 o'clock."

I leaned over my coffee cup and whispered to Phil. "Can you hear what those cops are saying?"

"Just a word every now and again," she said. I looked down at my coffee cup and concentrated on the conversation at the counter.

"Are y'all looking for somebody in particular?" the waitress asked the detectives.

"Radio traffic says it's a fair-complexioned guy about six feet. Medium build. Sharp nose with combed-back black hair. Dark suit, white shirt, dark tie. He might be in a white Mustang."

"You seen him?" joked the other detective.

"I ain't seen much of nobody the last two hours," the waitress said.

"Shooter allegedly registered in a flop house under an assumed name and took the shot from a second-floor window. Some kind of hunting rifle was found on the sidewalk outside. That's about all we know now." The detective sipped his coffee.

The waitress continued to wipe the counter and then reached under the large iron griddle to cut off the gas.

"My boss called a few minutes ago and said to go on and shut this place down if it looked like the curfew was going to take," the waitress said. "I reckon I'll plan on that . . . if I can even find a key. I've never known the doors on this place to be locked."

The waitress looked at the full coffee pots and then to the detectives.

"If y'all got a Thermos, I'll fill it up for you," she said.

The waitress looked over at us. "Last call for coffee. You young folks better be thinking about getting on home your own selves."

Thinking about it is all I was doing and getting nowhere. There was no home.

Phil stacked our coffee mugs on my plate and put everything on the counter for the waitress. "Well, thank you, hon. I 'preciate that," the waitress said. "I can tell you done some waitressing by the way you stack plates."

Phil nodded a smile at her and turned to the policemen on the stools. Though I was getting accustomed to Phil's surprises, her next words stunned me.

"We're from out of town and we're curious if it might be possible to make it to Coldwater, Mississippi, tonight. Maybe bend that *couvre-feu* a little?" Certain American words sounded better when she coated them with her French-Cajun accent.

The detective nearest to Phil smiled. He swiveled his stool toward her.

"Young lady, I'd say Coldwater is a good place to be about now, especially for somebody from South Louisiana."

Phil, surprised at the detective's comment, studied him more closely. He winked at her. "My wife's from Terrebonne Parish. I'd know that accent of yours anywhere."

"Plaquemines Parish," Phil said, slapping a hand on the counter. "All right, then. Which might be the best way for us to get ourselves to Coldwater?"

The other detective weighed in.

"Bellevue turns into Highway 51. Coldwater is 'bout 40 miles south," he said. "If you're in that little convertible out there, I'd put the top up and stay on the main streets. Wouldn't stop until I got all the way into Coldwater. Shouldn't be much street mischief going on there."

"You okay on gas?" the second detective asked. "All stations I know of are closed."

Phil glanced at me, and I nodded.

"Then let's get," she said. "Thanks, Mr. Policemans. You be watching yourself out there tonight."

The waitress stood at the cash register counting bills and change.

"How m-m-much for the coffee and hash browns?" I asked.

"You just had our curfew special, son," she said, without interrupting her counting. "It's on the house."

I mumbled a thank you and followed Phil out to the car closely.

"Ain't you even going to leave that nice lady a tip, Mr. Moneybags?" Phil asked me, but I didn't answer her because I had something else troubling me.

"I know the way to Coldwater," I said, as we stood at the car. "But . . . why did you t-t-tell that cop we're going there?"

"Isn't that where your Nellie Avant lives, the woman you went on so much about in your letters . . . the woman that you called 'Mam' and who you said pretty much raised you?" Phil was smiling. "You carried on so much about her in your letters, I had in mind I wanted to meet her anyway. Maybe she could see fit to put us up for the night . . . since we can't stay at your fancy-pants college."

I couldn't begin to come up with the words to explain all the reasons that going to Coldwater, Mississippi, to see Nellie Avant was a bad idea.

How could I explain to Phil that I had not seen Nellie in eight years? I couldn't explain it to myself. I knew Nellie Avant's mailing address in Coldwater, but I had never visited her. The last time I had seen Nellie was just before my mother took her to catch a Greyhound bus. I had failed to mention that little fact to Phil, also. I realized for the first time that for the past eight years, Nellie Avant, as much as I had thought about her and what she might be doing, resided only in a restrictive time capsule in my head.

36

Phil helped me put up the ragged top on the car. The worry-haints were circling again and making it clear to me that I needed to find a way to tell Phil a lot of things that were going to be uncomfortable for me. I didn't know where to begin. Only that I must.

CHAPTER 3

THE STREETS of downtown Memphis near the hospitals and the rambling buildings of the medical school were pleasantly quiet on my way to work in the early morning hours, but at just before 8 o'clock on a Thursday night, a time the streets should be buzzing with traffic, the emptiness was unnerving. Street signals on Union Avenue, the main east-west thoroughfare, calmly changed from red to green and back to red without cars crossing at the intersections.

The midtown streetlights seemed brighter, like somebody had forgotten to turn them off when they left an empty room.

I had in mind another way to Coldwater. I would take Highway 61 from downtown and then switch over to Highway 51 when I got to Whitehaven. For the moment, I guess, I was in fact going to Coldwater, Mississippi, no matter how impractical and useless it seemed.

As I neared the newspaper offices at 495 Union, I shifted to another plan that might give me some time to think about how I could tell Phil that we shouldn't be going to Nellie Avant's house in Mississippi.

"I need to leave a quick note for the newspaper's day side," I said to Phil as I pulled into the parking lot. "I'll leave the car running, you can l-l-lock the doors and I'll be right back."

"Thank you, but *non*," she said. "No way you're leaving me all cozy here in this little doodle with its raggedy-ass top and fire bombings going on. If you're going in, I'm going with you."

"But . . . ."

38

"Don't go buttin' with me," Phil said. "Let's get if we're gettin'."

In my side mirror I saw a white *Press-Scimitar* staff car pull into the lot. One of our photographers got out, popped the trunk and grabbed his canvas camera bag. The photographers had started using the smaller 35mm single-lens cameras instead of the heavier twin-lens models. Their camera bags were full of interchangeable lenses of different lengths, which made the bags hanging on their shoulders heavy to carry.

"We're lucky," I said to Phil. "I won't need to go up to the n-n-newsroom after all. I'll give the note to a photographer."

I put my reporter's notebook on the torn top of the car and scribbled with a pen:

> *National Guard arriving sometime tomorrow at Southwestern –* Vic.

I ripped the page out of the notebook and handed it to the photographer.

"Can you g-g-give this to the city desk?" The photographer nodded an okay.

"Wait." I grabbed the note back. I crossed out "tomorrow" and wrote "Friday" and handed the note back. One of the first lessons learned in the newsroom was that in a 24-hour news operation, the words "today" and "tomorrow" are ambiguous.

"How is it out there?" I asked the photographer.

"They had me shooting downtown fires and street-gangs," he said. "Almost got a brick through my windshield. Shot from the car window mostly. No need to risk it." From my first day on the job, I liked how the photographers said they "shot photos," a more pro-active verb. They never "took pictures."

The photographer stuffed my note in his shirt pocket and disappeared into the building.

"Did he say 'street gangs'?" Phil asked when I got back in the car. I nodded.

"All right," she said. "Coldwater, Mississippi, here we come . . . let's get."

Phil was the confident master of her domain in South Louisiana, even in a hurricane, but she was now in a strange city and one that appeared to be under siege.

"We'll be okay," I said, "b-b-but there's some things I n-n-need to tell you . . . as soon as I get a chance."

Phil gave me a quizzical look, which was justified. I was terrible at starting conversations that were going to be problematic for me, but I was going to have to come up with something. The air outside was crisp and cool but my palms were moist on the steering wheel.

THE MAIN STREETS of downtown Memphis were deserted with only the occasional police car or fire truck going by with sirens wailing. The large Malco theater marquee at the corner of Main Street and Beale with all its lights that would normally be twinkling was dark.

The side streets had the most activity. Not so many cars but plenty of people standing and talking on the sidewalks. I slowed to a stop after I turned south on Second Street. A half-block ahead of us a dozen or so young Black men walked in the middle of the four-lane street. Some carried metal pipes and one poked the air above his head with what looked like a tire iron.

"You sure know how to show a girl an exciting evening," Phil said, staring straight ahead.

"S-s-sorry."

"Instead of being sorry, you best be thinking of a way to get us out of this mess," Phil said. "I'm okay with gators and hurricanes, but I don't know about all this *couillon* craziness going on up here, sure."

Phil's eyes swept the scene in front of us. I had seen how she could handle herself in the wild swamps of Louisiana and on a powerful river in a small skiff, but she had let me know that this was not her element. She showed no fear, but her heightened awareness was evident. I clicked the high beam on my headlights for a better view of the streets.

"Cut 'em back down to low, Vic," Phil said. "We don't need to be calling attention to ourselves." I switched back to low beams.

In the distance, the sound of breaking glass echoed off buildings. We couldn't tell from which directions the erratic sounds were coming. A light haze of acrid smoke covered the streets.

"Keep it slow until we get to a cross street, then take it right or left, whichever way looks open," Phil said. "We need to get off this main *rue* quick like."

Downtown Memphis was a maze of one-way streets, which I knew well from my copy clerk runs to the post office and other government buildings. My little convertible, raggedy top and broken down as it was, was more responsive than the newspaper's old and clunky staff cars. I zigged and zagged around corners as Phil stared into the darkness.

"Don't go down any street where you see something on fire," Phil said. Her eyes darted back and forth, just as they had in her skiff on the violent Mississippi River when she was taking me out of harm's way three years ago as Hurricane Betsy bore down on us.

"How much farther to the Mis-sippi line?" she asked, without looking at me. I sometimes cut syllables out of long words for ease of pronunciation. Phil did it for expediency.

"Only a couple of miles," I said. "The city thins out quick after Crump Boulevard."

"I wouldn't pay much mind to red lights," Phil said. "Ease on through 'em. Don't think the police will be interested in writing any traffic tickets tonight."

Phil pronounced "po-lease" in two distinct syllables. Just like Nellie.

ON THE LAST DAY I saw Nellie Avant in Memphis in 1960, just before my mother took her to the bus station, she gave me a slip of paper with the address of her daughter's house in Coldwater, Mississippi, and said I could write to her there if I ever had a mind to.

My mother had asked me to go with her to take Nellie to the bus station on her last day for her trip back to Mississippi, but I made up some excuse to get out of it. I knew how much it would upset me to see Nellie leave on a bus. I did not understand why she had to go in the first place. My mother explained that there was no place for her to live at our new house in East Memphis. Our old house in midtown had an apartment over the garage where Nellie stayed. I had told my mother that my new room was plenty big and she could sleep there on one of my twin beds.

"Don't be ridiculous, Vic," my mother had scolded me. "I know how much you like Nellie, but she has to go back home to Mississippi."

The first year I typed letters to Nellie about how junior high school was going and how much I hated our new house in East Memphis, especially the new central-vacuum system with the long hose that my mother showed off to anybody who came to the house and would listen. And that my mother would never let me open the windows because the whole-house air conditioning would come on.

"Opening windows lets the air out," my mother would say, even though I viewed it as letting the air in, but I didn't argue much with my mother—or anybody else—when I was a teenager.

I continued to write letters to Nellie about starting high school, about getting my driver's license, and I told her about how much I liked playing baseball. I didn't tell her much about my other high school teams because I knew that baseball was the only sport that she cared anything about. My father had brought her to one of my Little League games when I was young. "Hit that ball hard, Number Four," I could hear her yell from the stands.

Not long after I began college at Southwestern, I started several letters to Nellie that talked about how I discovered that the man I had known to be my father was not my biological father, but I couldn't make the words come out like I thought they should for Nellie. I tore up the letters.

I did write her later on about meeting Phil on my trip to Louisiana, but I didn't say anything about being in the hurricane and almost drowning in the river because I knew it would worry her. I made sure to sign my letters with the name Nellie called me from the first day she came to live with us—Little Man.

Even though I typed my letters, I had my suspicions that Nellie couldn't read them all that well. The only book I ever saw her with was her Bible, and while she could turn to any story that she wanted in any book of the Bible, she essentially quoted from the story and didn't read the verses word for word even though she would follow along with her fingers.

The only return letters I got were a few short ones from her daughter, who wrote in her neat hand that Nellie liked hearing from me and that her mother was doing fine. In one of the letters from her daughter, I learned that they had moved to a house with a new address. I still had the address in my billfold, but I had not written for at least two years. And now, out of the blue, that's where Phil and I were headed. Or rather, where Phil was taking me. Phil might have seen our trip as a retreat from the violence in Memphis. I could not get the irritable thought out of my head that the worry-haints were somehow taking me to my punishment.

BOTH OF US relaxed somewhat after we crossed the state line. Everything felt more normal along Highway 51 as it became rural.

I needed to come clean with Phil on many fronts. She should know the real reason I couldn't fix the top on my car or stay in a regular dorm room. I was dead broke. I had written her about my parents' divorce, about my father starting his accounting business over again in New Orleans, but I had not mentioned what bad shape my finances were in. For one thing, I would feel silly complaining to Phil about not having any money. Her family's house had been destroyed by the hurricane. She had worked as a waitress and then she wrote me saying she had gotten a second job to help pay for the rebuilding of the house. She had learned how to fuel helicopters and look after them after their flights out to the new oil-drilling rigs being built in the Gulf of Mexico. Her two younger brothers had fixed up an old truck and started a trash pickup business after school before they were even old enough to get their driver's licenses. She wrote me once how much her two younger sisters enjoyed "going to the store," which was the parish community closet where a used dress or a pair of jeans might cost 50 cents.

With as few words as possible and with every intention of letting her know I was not feeling sorry for myself, I caught Phil up on the sorry state of my finances. I tried to make it sound like it was not a big deal to me, but she read more into my words.

"So how does it feel to scrape and claw for money like the rest of us, Sporty Boy?"

I had liked it when she called me "Sporty Boy" in the past, but the name now felt like she was mocking me. Getting into an argument with Phil was not a good idea, but I wanted to try to hold my own against her razor-whetted words.

"It's new to me, but old Sporty B-B-Boy will get the hang of it," I said.

When I tried to put added inflection in my words, my stutter ruined it, but she knew she had touched a nerve.

"Listen to me good now, Vic. The one reason I came up here this weekend was to see you . . . to talk to you *face à face*. You know I don't give a rip about your fancy college parties . . . and while we're both laying all our cards face up, I had the notion you invited me up here anyway just so you could show off your Louisiana girl, you know, the one you told your friends could out-dance anybody in Memphis and the one who chased swamp rabbits."

I recalled typing those exact words to her in a letter.

"Not . . . not s-s-show you off, but . . . you know . . . have the guys meet a real . . . ."

"A real what?" Phil said.

I didn't know how to finish my sentence.

"A real 'Cajun Queen'," she said. She had me dead to rights.

"Pl-pl-please, Phil, don't talk like that," I said. "I thought you understood me b-b-better than that." I might just as well have admitted that she understood me too well.

"I'm not sure what to understand about you," she said. "We had to get thrown off campus before you told me how bad off you were on money . . . and you wouldn't even let me buy my own train ticket up here 'cause you're Mr. Big Spending Fancy College Frat Boy."

Phil had a full head of steam. I knew better than to try to interrupt her.

"You told me your parents' divorce was no big deal to you. I think the *contraire* is true. You don't trust me enough to talk the truth to me. You're not the Vic I saw on that bridge . . . the one I saw turning over Mr. Spiro's ashes to the river."

The late Constantine Spiro, in a roundabout way, was the man responsible for me going to Louisiana and meeting Phil. I got to know the retired merchant marine and autodidactic scholar while I was helping Rat out on his newspaper route in the summer of 1959. Mr. Spiro and I became close as we discussed his travels around the world and his love for books and studying them. He was the only person, besides Rat, whom I could talk to about my stutter. His last request of me was to spread his ashes at the "mouth of the Mississippi River." My parents refused to let me go, but I slipped off from home for four days and ran into both Philomene Moreau and Hurricane Betsy. I had first thought the trip was for Mr. Spiro, but then I realized he had devised it for my benefit. To get me out of my comfort zone and to see the world—or at least another part of it—on my own.

Phil was right that I didn't feel like that same person standing on the bridge in New Orleans three years ago.

When my head was bashed in from falling out of Phil's boat and I was being carried away into the Gulf by the wild current of the Mississippi, I heard Mr. Spiro 's voice telling me not to fight the current because the current would always win.

I wasn't sure what current I was fighting now, but I knew too well that I was losing ground.

"Okay, so now you know I'm b-b-broke and that your weekend in Memphis is ruined . . . so I'm gonna let you in on something else," I said.

My eyes were on the highway, but I could feel Phil's eyes burning in on me as I got ready to deal with those miserable worry-haints.

"I haven't seen Mam . . . I mean, I haven't seen N-N-Nellie Avant in eight years . . . since she left Memphis. I know her d-d-daughter's new address in Coldwater, but that's all I know," I said. "And it's been a while since I wrote her, so I don't even kn-kn-know if that address is any good."

Silence stoked itself in the wind-ravaged car with the ragged top. Phil was loading up for me. I dared not look her way. I didn't have to wait long.

"You beat the band, Mr. Victor Vollmer. You been writing me in your letters how much you loved your 'Mam' and how she called you 'Little Man,' what all she did for you, how she taught you all those rhymes to get you to talk better, how much you write to her, how much she means to you and now you tell me you ain't even seen her since she left Memphis, what is it now, going on eight years?"

Phil waited for a response. When I offered none, she continued.

"That cop said Coldwater was forty miles away. It's not like it's on the other side of the damn moon, Vic. What on God's good earth do you mean treating a person like that? I'm *embarrassée* and feel sorry for Nellie Avant . . . and I've never even met the lady."

I had no rebuttal. I couldn't explain it myself. Too busy at school. Too busy working. Too busy going to fraternity parties. Too busy thinking about myself. Too busy worrying about my own problems. Too busy writing words that didn't amount to anything. Then tearing them up and throwing them away. Too busy trying to make believe I was somebody I was not.

"Phil . . . I'll find a p-p-place for us to spend the night, even if we have to go back to the newspaper. I've seen some cots in one of the storage rooms," I said. "I'll take care of it."

"You don't need to be worrying about me and about 'taking care of it,' " Phil said, mocking me. "You need to be worrying about growing up and acting like . . . ."

I couldn't imagine the words coming next, but I knew they would cut like the wire fishing line pulled taut by a deep-sea rod and reel. She paused, circled back and then let go.

"You're twenty-one years old, Vic. You're not 'Little Man' anymore," Phil said. "You need to stop acting like an *enfant* . . . a damn child, if you need me to translate."

In this roller coaster of a conversation, Phil had transitioned from *my girl* into my accuser. The words hurt but the silence began to hurt more.

48

THE SIGN at the one stoplight in Coldwater, Mississippi, pointed left: City Hall – Tate County Sheriff – One Block.

"Somebody ought to be in the sheriff's office who can give us directions," Phil said. There were no two ways about it. She was determined for us to find Nellie Avant. This was my part of the world and I needed to be doing the leading, but I was the one being led.

A light was on in the one-story brick building. I pulled into one of three open spaces in front of the building, next to a Tate County sheriff's cruiser.

"I'll go in," Phil said in her charter-boat captain's voice. "Just give me that last address you have for Nellie."

I had to regain my balance and find a way to get back to some kind of solid footing with Phil. The words "stay here" would be no problem as I plotted them out in my head, but those words wouldn't work for Phil, be they stuttered or sputtered. Phil reached for the passenger-side door handle, but I jumped out on my side ahead of her without speaking and sprinted to the building before she could get out of the car.

The front door was locked, but lights were on inside. I knocked on the frame of the door and then on the plate glass of the door, loud enough to make the door rattle on its hinges.

A large white man in a wrinkled sheriff's deputy uniform appeared at an interior doorway. His shirttail was out, and he was in his stocking feet. He came to the glass door.

"What'd'ya want?" The words were muffled by the thick glass.

"I need directions," I said, holding up the slip of paper with the address on it I had taken from my billfold.

The deputy came closer to the glass and looked outside. He motioned for me to step to one side. He looked both ways from behind the heavy glass door.

"Just a minute," he said.

 I watched him through the glass door. He returned with his shoes on, a ring of keys and unlocked the door.

Standing in the doorway, I explained that I was looking for the address on Arkabutla Dam Road.

"What you want out there this time of night?" he asked.

"We're looking for somebody. Her name is Nellie Avant."

"Where you from?" The deputy looked past me to Phil in the car.

"We're from Memphis . . . and we're trying to find N-N-Nellie Avant's house," I said. I was working extra hard to control my stutter.

"Don't know nobody out there by that name," he said. "What you want with somebody way out there after dark?"

The words "she's a friend of mine" sounded hollow and inappropriate at 9 p.m. in front of the sheriff's office in Coldwater, Mississippi, especially coming from a college-aged white boy in penny loafers. I reached into my back pocket for my wallet and pulled out my faded press card that I had used once or twice to enter a parking lot of a government building. My name typed on the card was smudged and barely legible.

"I'm with the *Press-Scimitar*," I said, with all the authority I could muster.

50

"Need to see some other ID," the deputy said. I showed him my driver's license. He looked back and forth at them, matching the names.

"What does a Memphis newspaper want with this woman . . . and at this time of night and with all the mess going on in the city?"

"I'm a ph-ph-photographer . . . a staff photographer . . . and the reporter in the car has been assigned to do a story on this woman . . . and her family," I said. I regretted over-explaining that I was a staff photographer. Lying and stuttering did not go together well because a lie needed to be spoken with confidence.

"What kind of story?" he asked. "Only Blacks live out there on that road."

"Not sure. Just some kind of a f-f-feature story, I guess. I'm just along to shoot the photos . . . you know . . . for the n-n-newspaper."

He looked at Phil in the car. Right on cue, she smiled and waved at the deputy.

"That little convertible you're in ain't no newspaper car," he said.

"It's my p-p-personal car. With all the news going on in Memphis, all the staff cars were taken," I said. I sounded almost believable. Maybe I could get the hang of telling a lie after all.

"Did y'all just come from Memphis?"

I nodded.

"How is it up there?" he asked. The deputy's tone made me think I was finally gaining some kind of purchase in our conversation.

"A few fires and street gangs . . . and the police chopper was shot at," adding the last bit of information in an attempt to shore up my credibility.

"Yeah, I heard that from state dispatch," the deputy said. "I'm supposed to be home in bed, but I guess I'll be sleeping here tonight with the two-way."

"Anything going on here?" I asked, in what I tried to pass of as the voice of a real news photographer. He said he hadn't heard of anything and began to give me directions to the address on Arkabutla Dam Road.

I held up my hand. "Can you hold on a minute?" I said. "I need to get my notebook from the car." The same one I had used to write my daily paragraph on middling spot cotton, whatever that was. I had heard Chis, the assistant managing editor at the newspaper, tell a summer intern one time that a reporter without a pen and notebook was like a gunfighter without bullets. I wasn't a reporter, but I was rarely without my notebook close by.

I SLID BACK into the driver's seat.

"I found out where Nellie lives," I announced triumphantly. "It's only about 15 minutes away."

"Don't count your chickens," Phil said. "We're not there yet."

Conversation was non-existent as we drove the dark roads. Phil finally broke the silence.

"Look, Vic, I'm sorry about going off on you a while ago," she said. "You remember when Daddy called me a 'Miss Queen Bee in short shorts' on that morning before we went out on the river. That hurt me to the marrow of my bones, but I came to realize how much truth there was in what he said, the way I strutted around Venice like a peafowl."

I remembered that morning in Louisiana well.

"You told me then that the ones who love you the most are the ones that will tell you what you don't want to hear," she said, settling back in her seat. "I guess that's all I'm saying."

The more I dissected her sentence and rolled it around in my head, the more I liked it. *The ones who love you the most.* Those were the exact words that had come from her mouth. I had lost hope that she could be *my girl*, but maybe I had been given a reprieve. Was she saying in some roundabout way that she might love me? Then I remembered that trying to sort out a conversation was dangerous when the busy-body worry-haints were circling in my head.

Chapter 4

THE WINDING Arkabutla Dam Road was darker than Highway 51 by a good measure.

I clicked on my high beams to discover in the awkward darkness that only one side of the high-beam lights was working. Another casualty of poor car maintenance due to my lack of funds.

The deputy had said not to bother looking for house numbers on mailboxes, just to take the first driveway on the left after passing the hulking two-story cotton gin that we couldn't miss even in the darkness.

We couldn't see a house at the end of the gravel driveway but took it anyway through a grove of young trees. My cock-eyed headlights eventually shone on a one-story brick house, small but well-kept, with trimmed shrubs along the front. A white Chevrolet, four or five years old, was parked in the carport with Tate County, Mississippi, license plates.

"This looks pretty nice," I said, trying not to sound too relieved. "I'm glad Nellie has a nice place."

"We don't know that for a *garantie*," Phil said. "Remember what they say about dem chickens that ain't hatched yet." Phil could pronounce "them" as well as anybody, but "dem chickens" in her South Louisiana patois was for my benefit.

I pulled in behind the Chevrolet. We could see the flickering lights of a television through the thin curtains on the big picture window.

54

"Cut the car off, but leave the headlights on," Phil said. "I'll go knock."

"No, let me," I protested. She held up that commanding hand again.

"Look, with everything that's going on, it's better a *fille* goes knocking on a strange house at night in the middle of Mississippi," Phil said. "We don't know for sure we got the right place. Just sit yourself tight." I couldn't argue with her assessment.

Phil slid out of the car, leaving the door open, and climbed the three brick-lined steps to the concrete porch. She rang the doorbell. A porch light came on and then the door cracked.

A Black woman who appeared to be middle-aged, too young to be Nellie, opened the storm door and Phil stepped inside. I pushed my wristwatch closer to the weak dashboard lights—11 minutes after 10.

Then 20 minutes after 10.

The lights from the television in the house continued to pulsate behind the curtains. The 10 o'clock news, probably from a Memphis station, might still be on. Part of the mystique of working at a newspaper is that you seemed to know at any moment what was going on in your city and then in the rest of the world from all the news coming in over the wires. Sitting in the black night on a gravel driveway in North Mississippi felt like I was underwater again in the river. Out of touch with all that must be happening in Memphis and around the world. The street protestors and the fires in Memphis had disturbed me. Frightened me, to be truthful, but I had this other gnawing feeling that I had abandoned my post. I had in mind one day that I could be an assured reporter, but now found myself sitting in my car in front of a strange house in the dark Mississippi night without a clue of what might be happening around me.

I unfastened my watch from my arm to get a closer look at the hands and decided at exactly 10:30 I would go up and ring the doorbell and at that moment the front door of the small house opened and then the storm door. Phil was smiling. She motioned for me to get out of the car. I fumbled to put my watch back on as I opened the door.

"Vic, this is Nellie's daughter, Bernice," Phil said, when I got to the porch steps.

I thought back to the short notes I had gotten from the daughter. They were written in a neat cursive hand. She had signed them only with the letter "B." When Nellie had lived with us, she had talked about a daughter some, but as far as I could remember, she had never called her by name.

"I'm glad to m-m-m . . . ." Before I could finish my sentence, Nellie's daughter smiled and wrapped her outstretched arms around me in a warm embrace.

"Miss Nellie will be so glad to see you, Little Man," Bernice said. "She talks about you and the good times y'all had in Memphis to this very day."

"Isn't she here?" I asked in bewilderment. "Is ev-everything okay?"

Bernice explained that Nellie had wanted to go back to live in the house where she was raised even though Bernice managed, with her mother's help, to move into a more modern house.

"Living inside a house made of tight bricks just didn't feel right to Mama," Bernice said. "Now she can walk to her small church from the old homeplace. We try to get her to move in with us, but she allows as how she is the happiest there."

Bernice's smile reminded me of Nellie's. Genuine and inquisitive.

56

"The government did us a right good favor when they put in the new dam and levee system," Bernice said. "That old Mississippi would have washed Mama's old homeplace away for sure without that levee."

"Bernice gave me directions on how to get there," Phil said. "It's only about ten minutes from here in the car."

Phil then turned to Bernice. "Maybe you can call her and tell her we're on the way?"

"Mama don't have a phone," Bernice said. "I offered to put one in and get her a TV and an antenna, but she said that she didn't want any of that foolishness. All she needed was her old table radio."

"Wonder if she'll still be up when we get there?" Phil asked.

"Don't matter about that. I know she'll want to see you . . . Little Man."

Little Man? That person now seemed like a vague acquaintance from my past, but it was comforting to hear the name again that reminded me of the comfortable home I once had in which Nellie Avant was such an important part.

"Remember, now, if you get to where the levee ends, you've gone too far," Bernice said to Phil. "Miss Nellie probably won't have the lights . . . ." Bernice stopped in mid-sentence and started up her steps. "You two just wait here for me to put a coat on over my robe and get my car keys. Y'all don't need to be traipsing around that Coldwater River in the pitch dark. You can just follow me out there."

I RECALLED a story from the *Press-Scimitar* that told about the creation of Arkabutla Lake in the 1940s when the Coldwater River was dammed by the U.S. Corps of Engineers. The levee and dam were in response to the Great Flood of 1927. The new lake—along with new impoundments at Enid, Grenada and Sardis—was supposed to help with flooding problems on the lower Mississippi River. Nellie had told me stories about growing up on Coldwater Creek that flowed into the Coldwater River. I had asked her if the water actually was cold. "Not any more than most," she had said. "But it was dark. Dark, deep and not to be trifled with. That's where they got the 'cold' from."

We followed the taillights of the white Chevrolet on Arkabutla Dam Road for a few miles and then turned onto a gravel road, not so much a driveway but more of a construction road. The gravel rocks were large and loose. I could feel my lightweight car slide and then the rear wheels spin in the gravel if I turned the steering wheel too quickly.

The Chevrolet slowed and then turned left, not onto a driveway but over a culvert and into what looked like a field. Bernice's high beams came on. In front of us was a small wooden house with a hodge-podge roof. A stove pipe with a triangle of a cap at its top jutted through the roof at an odd angle, supported by a single wire. The house may have been painted white at one time but not lately.

My relief in first thinking that Nellie Avant lived in a modern brick house now turned into a horror, a bleak scene that set the worry-haints to buzzing again. Nellie was the one who had first told me about the "haints" and to never let them get the best of me. They were having a field-day inside me now as I surveyed the dismal scene illuminated by headlights.

The house in front of me could be described only as a shack, and a disheveled one at that. The roof looked as if one portion of it was shingled but then I realized it was a tin roof with parts of it dark from years of rust. The wooden front porch was not level with the house. The windows were crooked in the walls of the shack, like drawings in a cartoon.

Bernice left her car running with the headlights on. She went to the porch and knocked and then just opened the screen door and walked in. Interior lights came on quickly. I started to say, "At least she has electricity," but I kept my mouth shut. A dull porchlight, a single naked bulb by the door, came on.

In the pale illumination, I recognized Nellie Avant's quick gait as she came out on the porch and down the steps ahead of Bernice. I recognized the white sleeping cap she wore and the flannel night gown with its various patches. I recognized in a whole way the wonderful woman I had always thought of as my best friend but whom I had ignored for eight years except for a few typed letters that all felt shallow and wanting as I watched the scene unfold before me. Mr. Spiro had explained to me once that the emotions of happy and sad are not on the opposite ends of the spectrum but are, in truth, dramatically close to each other. At that moment, the weight of both descended upon me.

I jumped out of my car. Nellie and I embraced. I didn't want to let go of her. I wanted the hug to last forever and wanted it to wipe away the last eight years. I choked back my throaty sobs with all the expertise I had gained from dealing with speech blocks for most of my life. A life given over to trying to hide a stutter also gave a person a leg up when trying to hide emotions.

PHIL WALKED Bernice to her car. I wanted to thank her for reuniting me with Nellie, but I was having trouble finding the words—always a problem, but more of a problem when emotions had overtaken me. I knew Phil would share my thanks. I followed Nellie into her house. I noticed that either I had grown taller or Nellie had shrunk since I last saw her. But I could not tell that she had changed much in the eight years since I had seen her, except for more gray hairs peeking out from under her night cap.

A wood stove sat in the back of the front room. A shiny sheet of tin had been tacked to the wall behind the stove. Nellie opened the stove door to expose a bed of dying embers.

"You don't even have a coat on in the chill of this night," Nellie said. "I'll stoke this fire up for us."

She threw in a few sticks of firewood from a black bucket. I had not thought about the chill. Phil had put on a light rain jacket that had been wadded up in her bag while I was talking to the photographer at the newspaper. The one jacket I had was back in the fraternity house on the campus that we had been turned away from.

"Let me get on a proper housecoat," Nellie said. "I be back directly." She disappeared into a back room.

Phil was still outside with Bernice. I was glad for some time alone to get my thoughts under control. What I saw in the dim light thrilled me. Nellie's needle stories. They were draped on both arms of an old sofa, rested on small tables and were tacked randomly on the wall.

Watching Nellie work on her needle stories with colored thread had always mesmerized me. She would talk about what she was creating as the needle moved in and out of the cloth in an almost magical motion. Most scenes were stories from the Bible, but she would occasionally conjure a representation from her childhood. The needlework pieces were all new to me except for a large one that I recognized tacked on the wall behind the sofa that showed animals going into Noah's Ark, two at a time. She would usually take that one with her to work on when we went to the Overton Park Zoo in Memphis, adding representations of different animals with her colorful threads on every visit.

60

The gas stove against a back wall in the kitchen was old and small. I had seen a rusty propane tank outside when we drove up. The cupboards had curtains for doors. A squatty refrigerator stood next to a dull-white porcelain sink that hung on the wall with its pipes exposed. A water heater stood in the corner with pipes reaching out like limbs of a tree. But everything was clean, just so and in its place. Just what you would expect in a house where Nellie Avant lived. Even if it was a broken-down shack in the wilds of the Mississippi delta.

I stood alone in the middle of the room as Phil came through the front door.

"You okay, Vic?" she asked. I nodded.

"Look at Nellie's needle stories," I said with excitement as I twirled around the room. "I think I t-t-told you about them."

"You did, sure. How she could sew her pictures and thread her needles with either hand."

Phil went to the ones on the wall and looked closely at them, gently tracing their lines with her fingers.

"Most look to be Bible stories," she said. "My mama did some embroidery, but these look all done freehand. No telling how long each one took her. Look at those *jolies couleurs*."

Nellie came into the room wearing a simple print dress instead of a housecoat. At first it seemed odd that she would have anything on except her starched white uniform, but I was still bouncing wildly between my memories and the present. She had on a pair of wire-rimmed glasses that I had not seen before.

"I had to get my new drugstore spectacles on to see this pretty girl here," Nellie said.

"This is Phil that I wrote to you about," I said. Nellie gave her a hug and then took both of Phil's hands and stepped back like they were dancing.

"Now, I know Little Man speaks of you as 'Phil,' but that can't be a right name for a pretty one like you."

"It's short for Philomene," Phil said, with the closest thing I had ever seen from her that could be called a blush.

"Now that's a beauty of a name that matches you," Nellie said. "Little Man wrote me about you and how much he liked getting to know you and talking with you on his trip down in Louisiana."

Talking.

The word stirred up memories and confusion. I found myself tempted to stutter more for Nellie, to show her I was still her Little Man, but another part of me was eager to show her that my speech had improved, maybe even with her help. That I could string several words together without too many blocks and hesitations and strange starter sounds that I once relied on. I focused hard on my next words, plotting them out in my head to make sure they came out smoothly.

"I'm still working at the newspaper . . . like I wrote you," I said.

"Now, good for you. How's your schooling going?"

"Okay, but I like working at the newspaper b-b-better than school."

"I guess y'all be busy up there at the paper with all the news about Dr. King," Nellie said, shaking her head. "My Sweet Jesus, hearing all that on the radio, I feel like I been shot through with a bullet my own self."

Neither Phil nor I could think of anything to say. Phil finally came through.

"It's right bad in Memphis, Miss Nellie," Phil said. "And that's one of the reasons we're here."

"But . . . not the only reason," I piped in. Phil shot me her unmistakable look of anger that she could manage so effectively. I decided I had it coming.

"I was supposed to put up at a dormitory at Vic's college in Memphis for the weekend, but everything got shut down on us," Phil said. "We were wondering if we might rest a little here before Vic has to go to work tomorrow. Everything is so crazy up in Memphis."

"You know you're plenty welcome here . . . but you might be more comfortable back at Bernice's. She has an empty room with her kids gone and she'd be glad to have you. It would be a mite warmer there."

So, Nellie had grandchildren. How could it be that I had never heard about them?

"On, no," I said. "Phil can s-s-sleep on the couch, and I can just maybe lie down on a bl-bl-blanket on the floor."

"That would do us nicely, Miss Nellie, if it wouldn't be too much trouble," Phil said.

"We can do a portion better than that," Nellie said, "but let me cook you something to eat. When's the last time y'all had something in your bellies?"

I was not sleepy and didn't think I was hungry after the hash-browns at the Toddle House until Nellie mentioned her cooking. I had been existing several semesters for the most part on saltine crackers and block cheese from the refectory at school. The school called it "government cheese" and wasn't supposed to serve it once the consume-by date had passed, so they would give it to any students who wanted it. I could make one sleeve of crackers and a hunk of cheese last for two days.

"We don't want to put you out any," Phil said.

"Ain't no puttin' out about it," Nellie said. "Them six hens I got out back been laying enough eggs for half of Tate County. Y'all make yourself at home while I heat up the stove."

PHIL RETRIEVED her bag from the car and changed into her red pajamas in Nellie's bedroom. The pajama top was not tucked into the bottoms. I looked to see if the little *fleur-de-lis* tattoo in the small of her back might be visible, but it was covered. Not a day had gone by in the last three years that I didn't think about that tattoo that I had discovered on her back but had never asked her about.

In less than half an hour, Nellie had spread out a meal for the two us. Scrambled eggs, strips of bacon, biscuits with butter and homemade blackberry jam. She was surprised when I told her I would take a cup of coffee if she had any.

"When did you learn to drink coffee, Little Man?" she asked.

"I guess in Louisiana," I said.

"What else you think you might have learned down there in Louisiana?" Nellie asked with her mischievous smile. Phil and I looked at each other, which started the three of us laughing. I had forgotten how Nellie's short sentences could contain volumes of insight and innuendo.

On the uncomfortable ride from Memphis to Coldwater, I didn't know what Phil would think of Nellie Avant, if we were even able to find her. I should have known that my favorite two people in the world would take to each other like long-lost family. Like they had known each other forever. Since my parents divorced, I had been without a real home. In this weather-worn shack in Tate County, Mississippi, not too far from the Tennessee state line and the Mississippi River, I felt the peace of home again.

My world, which had seemed so exciting when Phil got off the train, had started to tilt off its axis at a few minutes past 9 p.m. when someone shot Dr. Martin Luther King with a rifle at the Lorraine Motel. The night somehow began to feel salvaged now, and Nellie's fat buttermilk biscuits were never so delicious.

THE SLEEPING PLAN that Nellie laid out for us made sense.

The couch and several quilts would be mine. Nellie kept a thick pallet under her bed that she had used when Bernice's children would sleep over when they were young. Nellie said that Phil could sleep on that in her bedroom since there was a small electric space heater in there.

"I would love that," Phil said with a generous smile.

"Radio said it would get mite near freezing tonight," Nellie said.

The high temperature before the tornadoes came through just 24-hours before was 78 degrees but the fresh chill had come on quickly. A typical up-and-down spring in Memphis.

Nellie said I could take the radio she listened to in bed and plug it in at the outlet near the sofa. She said there might be news coming out of Memphis on "station 600" if I was of a mind to listen to it. I said I would like to do that. Like so many times when she lived with us in Memphis, Nellie seemed like she could think my thoughts before I had a chance to consider them.

Nellie was back in her night gown and sleeping cap when she came to tell me good night. She had a small flashlight in her hand, which she put on the table near the radio.

"If you're needing to do any business during the night, take this to the privy outback, through that back door in the kitchen . . . about thirty paces," she whispered. "You don't have to worry about no snakes in this cold weather. Anyhow, my old cuss-mean rooster keeps any crawling things away."

I nodded. She kissed me on the forehead.

"Goodnight, Little Man. You know, I's plenty happy to see you." She patted my foot like she had done so many nights in my upstairs room in Memphis. I did not smell the musty aroma of the Garrett's snuff that she once carried in her lower lip.

I needed a verbal cleansing of my own.

"I kn-kn-know I called you 'Mam' back in Memphis, but I think I should call you 'Nellie' now . . . if that's okay?" She stroked my forehead.

"I know you had to call me that 'cause it fit your sounds better," she said. "I was glad for you to call me whatever was the easiest for you."

"And I still like to hear you call me 'Little Man', but maybe calling me 'Vic' would be better," I said.

"That's all good and right," she said. "Names can change but we always are who we were. There's no changing that, is there?"

We always are who we were.

66

Had Mr. Spiro told me that during one of our talks? It sounded like one of his deep philosophical admonitions with which he liked to test me.

We always are who we were.

Was that an indictment or was it the turning of a page?

Even the mischievous worry-haints were going to have trouble with that one.

The flames in the cast-iron stove had died out, but the embers gave off a comfortable heat in the night's chill.

A privy. An outdoor bathroom. An outhouse. I had no idea. Why did I not know that the person who was so dear to me lived in a house, in the year 1968 no less, with no indoor toilet, no telephone and a woodstove for heat?

WREC-600 AM radio repeated what I already knew. The suspect in Dr. King's assassination was a white man in a dark suit driving a white Mustang. Memphis was under a strict curfew with roaming gangs of protestors and fire-bombings all over the city. The station then broke in with a national news feed about violence across the country, including New York City, Detroit and Tallahassee, Florida, where a white youth had been killed in a firebombing. Most governors in the South and Northeast had put their National Guard units on alert. The radio news signed off at midnight with the weather. The overnight low in Memphis would be 34—a 44-degree drop in temperature—and colder in the outlying areas.

I had been awake since going to work at three-thirty that morning, but I wasn't feeling the first signs of sleep. My mind raced with questions. What time would Phil and I need to leave the next morning for me to report to work at eight? How would I occupy Phil since she couldn't ride in a staff car with me? Would my fraternity's Old South Ball and the weekend festivities be cancelled due to the curfew? Probably. And why would somebody as famous as Dr. King choose to stay at a place like the Lorraine Motel instead of the Peabody Hotel in downtown Memphis where most famous people spent the night? What did Nellie think about me showing up on her doorstep in the middle of the night after being out of her life for eight years except for a few letters that now struck me as pitifully shallow? Why did Nellie have to live in a tumbled-down shack with no indoor bathroom?

The Mid-South night was clear after the tornadoes had cleaned out the clouds and humidity. Nellie had given me two quilts, but I still had on the clothes I had been wearing all day. I went to a window and looked at my watch in the moonlight—3:15 a.m. I tip-toed in my stocking feet over to the bedroom door to check on Phil. I could tell by the orange light from the small electric heater that the pallet on the floor was empty. I looked at Nellie's bed in the dim light and saw two lumps under the quilts. Nellie's white nightcap and Phil's black curls were just visible.

I laid back down on the sofa and pulled the quilts up over me. I felt myself trying to slip back into a battle with the worry-haints, but the sight of Nellie and Philomene in the same bed was enough to keep the haints away. My two favorite people in all the world were right there in the room next to me. No worry-haints could compete with the wonderment of that vision.

CHAPTER 5

April 5, 1968
Friday

A CROWING ROOSTER in good voice awakened me under Nellie's cozy quilts.

Then came the smell of coffee and the softness of whispers in the east light of the morning from the kitchen. I looked at my watch but the goop in my eyes made it hard to see the hands. Short sleep did not mean there was not deep sleep. I rubbed my eyes and checked the time again. A little after 6 o'clock. Two and half hours of sleep, but I felt rested.

Nellie and Phil were both dressed and standing near the stove. Phil turned to me.

"Good morning, *la belle au bois dormant*," she said. I had learned enough French from Phil and my brief stint in a college French class to figure out her luscious string of words meant "sleeping beauty." I could think of no better way to awaken than to a French idiom from Phil. A kind one.

Nellie and Phil both were the lucky types who seemed to go from sleep to wide awake in a few blinks of the eye. I had to move around before I could escape sleep's shroud.

"I'm fresh out of more biscuit fixin's," Nellie said to me from the stove, "but I got light bread, and I can make us some toast with cane molasses to dress it."

"That would suit me fine," I said. "And some coffee." I had noticed for the past several years that my stuttering also was affected by sleep. My fluency was the best in the early mornings when I wasn't fully awake, but the stuttering always came back into my life with the emerging light.

I slipped on my penny loafers. I started to say I needed to go outside to use the bathroom but decided it best to just go out the back door with no announcements.

Phil's plans, as usual, were in place and ahead of me when I came back into the house.

"I'm gonna just stay here and be with Nellie," Phil said. "You go on and do what you have to do at the newspaper and don't worry 'bout foolin' with me. I want to meet Miss Blythe anyway."

Phil was masterful at springing surprises on me.

"Miss B—Blythe?" One of the many speech therapists that my parents had sent me to in high school called the B-sound a "plosive," a challenge I feared almost as much as the V-sound. Even though inflection on the sound of the "B" was complicated by an extended stutter, I was satisfied my words came across as a question.

"She's a young'un from Tunica who spends the days with me some when there's no school for her," Nellie said. "I started on keeping her at her mama and daddy's big house, but she likes to come out here and mess with the chickens."

Phil completed the story.

"Nellie says she's been helping out, keeping her for several years," Phil said, "and I'm dying to meet Blythe after hearing Nellie tell me about her."

I wanted to ask what "helping out" meant, but I thought better. I wanted to ask how many days a week Nellie "helped out," but I thought better about that also. I wanted to ask if this meant Nellie was still working at a full-time job, but none of the questions sounded like the answers would gain me anything.

"How old is she?" I asked.

"Maybe going on 15," Nellie said.

Already conjuring up the mystery girl named "Blythe" in my head, I had pictured her as little more than a toddler and Nellie as possibly the babysitter.

"Shouldn't she be in school?" I asked.

"She goes to a special school in Senatobia but it's not every day like a regular learning school," Nellie said.

Phil saw my confusion. Perhaps she even recognized a hint of the jealousy that had sought me out from nowhere.

"I think Blythe may be in what my instructors call the 'special needs category,' " Phil explained.

"What kind of s-s-special needs exactly," I asked.

Nellie answered in her elemental way that explained more than labels.

"It just means she don't use her thinking like most young'uns her age. No better, no worse. Just different."

"She sounds like a lot of fun, and it will be nice to spend some time with her and get away from all that craziness in Memphis," Phil said. "And Vic won't have to spend the day worrying about me."

One of my questions from the night had been answered. Phil's decision to stay at Nellie's cut both ways with me. I didn't want to leave her, but I also didn't want her stuck in Memphis with nothing to do while I was busy going on the hectic film runs and sorting copy from the wires. Also, I didn't like the idea of her being around the inquisitive and aggressive reporters in the newsroom without me there. Without a doubt, she could take care of herself, but I wanted to have her all to myself. I knew my jealousy would overtake me if anybody in the newsroom started paying too much attention to her.

"Okay," I said. "I'm only scheduled to work 'til 2 o'clock, but I can try to get off sooner."

"Take your time," Phil said. "Nellie and I have a lot to do. And I can't wait to go out and see how many eggs that Blythe and I will gather this morning. We used to have chickens at home, but Mama would get upset every time we lost one on the road. She finally decided the best place for the chickens was in her gumbo."

I looked at Nellie at the stove, smiling.

The three of us sat down to coffee and toast made in the oven, browned just right on one side and covered in butter. The toast had been cut on the bias like all those many breakfasts in Memphis. The jar of molasses made a pop when Nellie twisted off the two-piece lid. My mother always enjoyed telling her friends that Nellie could open any jar that she could get her hand around, and she could do it with her right hand or her left hand.

"You can wash up in the basin in my room if you's needin' to 'fore you go to work," Nellie said.

I shook my head. "They have sh—showers at work, but I may have trouble getting to my clean clothes at school anyway," I said.

Nellie wasn't eating her toast. She stared at me as she sipped her coffee with the spoon still in the cup and her thumb hooked around it like always.

"Your words be coming out smoother now without those empty spaces, Little Man," Nellie said. "Oh, my sorry. I'm supposed to be calling you 'Vic.' "

She turned to Phil. "It's gonna take me some time to fall into calling my Little Man anything else, Miss Philomene. You knows that we always are who we once were."

There was that sentence again that seemed to go straight to my gut.

Nellie turned back to me and smiled. "I knew you'd find a way to make your words work better for you. It may not be exactly how you would wish it, but it's working just fine for you."

I was at a loss on how to respond. My mother and father rarely talked about my stuttering with me when I was growing up. Rat and Mr. Spiro were the only friends who I had ever managed to discuss it with—until Phil came along. Phil convinced me that I worried about my stutter more than I should. She likened my speech to more of a "sputter," similar to the sound made by the small outboard engine on her fishing skiff.

"Didn't we have us a time saying all those rhymes I taught you?" Nellie said.

My naïve thinking as a pre-teen had told me the playground rhymes Nellie had shared with me were just for fun, not realizing until she had left Memphis that saying the sing-song rhymes over and over was her crude method of speech therapy. I never stuttered when I repeated rhymes or sang. I wasn't sure the rhymes helped my speech, but it may have been just as effective as all my other sessions with the string of speech therapists my parents sent me to. And there was no doubt that the rhymes were more fun.

"You wanna do that 'Pullin the Skiff' for Miss Philomene?" Nellie asked. "That was our favorite."

Why not?

We performed the non-sensical rhyme with our usual hand-clapping gusto. Phil joined in on the rhythm, slapping her legs as she did a truncated two-step dance. I had work to do to get back on Phil's good side and the playground rhymes would help.

"I still have to work hard on my speech, especially at the n-n-newspaper," I said, after the rhyming and handclapping.

"All of God's beings have to work at something," Nellie said. "Chickens don't stop scratching. Cows don't stop giving. Work is what keeps us standing up straight."

I was beginning to realize that in her unique way, Nellie was just as much of a philosopher as my late friend, the self-educated Mr. Spiro, who was the one responsible for sending me to Louisiana where I was lucky enough to meet Philomene Moreau.

PHIL WALKED me to the car while Nellie cleared the breakfast dishes.

"I hate to l-l-leave you here . . . all alone," I said. "Are you sure you'll be okay today?"

Phil let out one of her laughs bathed in sarcasm.

74

"Oh, my stars in heaven," she said, fluttering her eyes and mocking. "How is this *petite fille* from Louisiana ever going to survive near this mean old Mississippi River. I just may get the swoons."

"Okay," I said. "I know when to let it alone."

"Nellie said that Blythe will be here about 9 o'clock . . . and we're going to have us a good day," Phil said with a genuine excitement. "You go on and do what you need to do at your newspaper."

I grabbed the towel that I kept behind my car's seat to wipe the dust off the windshield that had turned into a thin sheet of mud with the heavy delta dew.

"But I'm going to get b-b-back as quick as I can," I said, sliding into the bucket seat. "If the curfew is still on, we won't be going to the p-p-party, but I'll come up with something to make up for it."

Phil stuck her head in the window and lightly kissed my cheek.

"You don't need to be making up for anything, Sporty Boy," Phil said. "I'm looking forward to spending the day with Nellie."

Phil was sending me off to Memphis with a semblance of a kiss. Perhaps it was her way of trying to get us back to where I thought we belonged, and I appreciated that more than she could know.

THE GRAVEL ROADS of Mississippi again put a heavy film of dirt on my windshield. The washer mechanism also was busted on my car, another item to have fixed if I ever could manage to save the money.

I stopped when I reached the state line, pulled out my old towel and scraped at the windshield. I calculated that with the lack of traffic I would be at the newspaper at least a half-hour early. Since the Memphis airport was on the way to the newspaper, there would be time to check to see if our photographer who was supposed to be stationed there had any rolls of film that needed to be shuttled to the newsroom.

The photographer gave me a surprised look when I pulled up beside his staff car in the parking spaces reserved for the media.

"Have you got a two-way in that little car of yours?" the photographer asked through his open window. I shook my head.

"Man, I just this minute radioed in and the city desk said they would send you out as soon as you got in," he explained. "I just shot a roll of Attorney General Ramsey Clark arriving at Memphis Air. I don't think anyone else has it, even the TV stations." The photographer was excited about the exclusive shot he had managed to capture on film.

"It's too late for the Mid-South edition, but it should be good for the Home," the photographer said. "They told me to sit tight here in case anybody else important flies in."

He handed me the roll of film.

"This is 400 Tri-X. Tell Twist 'n Shout that he should push it to 1200," the photographer said. "He'll know what I'm talking about." Just as with middling spot cotton on the Memphis Exchange, I had no idea what any of the instructions meant, but I wrote them down in my notebook carefully.

The youngest staff photographer, who was pulling the tedious darkroom duty, had been declared "Twist 'n Shout" from his habit of singing and dancing while he agitated the exposed film in the cans of photo chemicals.

"Got it," I said. "You might r-r-radio the city desk and tell them I'm on the way in with your film." The photographer nodded.

My part in the coverage of the biggest story of the year—by far the biggest one of my three years at the newspaper—was meager, but I had made a good decision to stop at the airport on the way in. There would be time now for the news photo of the attorney general to make the main editions without any deadline issues.

I HANDED OFF the film to Twist 'n Shout with the instructions for developing and headed to the Teletype machines to see if the other copy clerks needed help when the city editor shouted at me across the newsroom.

"Vic, do you think you can get on the Southwestern campus?"

"I think so," I said, quickening my step.

"Good. We sent a reporter over there to interview somebody from the National Guard," the city editor said, "but they won't let us set foot on campus. It's a private school so they can keep us out."

I nodded.

"See if you can do any good over there."

"You mean . . . interview somebody?" I asked.

"Yes, interview somebody. Anybody. Soldiers, students, teachers. Whoever you can get to talk," he said. "And take a small 35 camera with you from photo. Don't let 'em see it or they may try to confiscate it. Shoot anything you can. Our reporter said the TV trucks couldn't get on campus either. If you get anything, you can call the story in to the city desk on the car radio and then rush the film back."

The scene at the guarded campus entrance played out in my mind.

"I should take my car," I said. "It's got a resident parking sticker on it . . . b-b-but that means I can't c-c-call the story in." Like I was capable of doing that anyway, I chastised myself.

"Don't worry about it," the city editor said. "Just get back as quick as you can. Copy deadline for the Home is 11:10."

"How 'bout the other film runs?" I asked.

"We're full for the Home," he said. "Hey, that was good thinking to stop by the airport on your way in."

The idea of having to "call in" a story to the rewrite desk over the radio horrified me. Conversational stuttering was something I was getting more comfortable with in the newsroom, but the idea of formally composing a story in my head and relaying it over a two-way radio would have the worry-haints tripping all over themselves. I had gotten it in my head that when I was writing that I actually thought with my fingers just as much as with my brain. It seemed my fingers needed to be moving to have cogent thoughts. My mouth might stutter on words, but my fingers never did.

THE CAMPUS GUARD who stepped out of the shack was one of the regular campus employees who recognized me. He had asked me to get him some of the government cheese any time the cafeteria was giving away extra. He came out with his clipboard.

"Let me get the number on your parking sticker," he said. "They're making us write everything down." I was glad I had put the newspaper's 35mm camera in my trunk.

"I see some National Guard trucks b-b-behind the gym. When did they get here?" I asked, in what I thought passed for an uninterested student's voice.

"Been coming in all the morning," the security guard said. I decided not to ask him any more questions, not wanting to tip my hand as an erstwhile reporter.

My fraternity house was the second closest one to the gym. I went to my unsanctioned attic room, got a change of clothes and my toothbrush. I took the camera out of my trunk and put it between the clean pants and shirt I was holding. To my surprise, students were playing pickup basketball games inside the gym at a time when they should have been in classes. I only had two subjects on Fridays, but I had told the professors in advance that I had made arrangements to get lecture notes because I was going to have to miss their classes.

"Hey, Vic. We need an extra. Go get your tennis shoes on," one of my fraternity brothers yelled.

"Got something else to do," I explained. "Shouldn't you b-b-be in class?"

"All cancelled," he said. "You probably heard that Old South has been called off too," he said, as he bounced the basketball. "Looks like we'll have to eat our deposit on the band . . . but we're gonna go on and pick up the kegs anyway."

"Too bad," I said, trying to dredge up some empathy, which seemed unusually difficult. Was I glad the once all-important Old South Ball had been called off? I decided I was.

I showered in the locker room and put on my clean shirt and pants, wrapping the camera in my dirty clothes. On my way out of the gym, I took the stairs up to the mezzanine level of the gym. I opened a casement window for a clear shot of the different types of military vehicles circled around large tents that were being erected. My hands shook. I rested the camera on the windowsill, framed the photo as best I could and snapped the shutter. Once. I had heard the photographers talk about "bracketing" shots with different camera settings, but I could only find the wherewithal to snap once and hope the shot was in focus.

I went back to my car and stowed my dirty clothes and the camera in the trunk.

NEWSPAPER REPORTERS normally identified themselves when they asked for an interview. "I'm so-and-so from the *Press-Scimitar* and I have a few questions . . . ."

Was I a real reporter? I didn't know if the campus authorities had barred the media or if it was the decision of the powers-that-be at the National Guard.

Two guardsmen who seemed as if they might be in charge of something stood near a jeep. I pulled my reporter's notebook from my back pocket and then realized that "Memphis Press-Scimitar" was printed on the cover. I flipped the cover over to hide the name.

"Got t-t-time for a few questions?" I said to the guardsmen. My attempt at sounding casual apparently fell short. The two uniformed men looked at each other.

"Not supposed to be any reporters in here. Who are you with?" the older one asked.

Decision time.

"I'm a student here. Just our campus newspaper. No b-b-big deal."

I could always explain I had meant to offer the story to the school newspaper, but then found out that a real newspaper wanted it. I was on the staff of the campus newspaper for a couple of semesters, but I had to quit when I started spending more time at work. The stories assigned to me were not interesting, anyway. Southwestern didn't have journalism courses, but I took all the rhetoric courses it offered, learning the basics of who, what, when, where and why.

The guardsmen were from counties in Middle Tennessee. I asked them to spell their names for me.

"You say you're with the campus newspaper?" the older one asked.

I nodded. "Classes are called off today. Need to be d-d-doing something."

They answered most of my questions. I threw in a few softball questions for good measure, so I would sound more like a college kid and not a real reporter.

I spotted a professor I had for British history and two students, whom I didn't know. The erudite professor called the unknown assassin a "scalawag." Was that a real word? I would need to check the spelling on that for the direct quote. The students were upset about the curfew and that the weekend parties had all been cancelled. I decided I had enough for the story.

My car was on something like autopilot as I drove back to the newspaper. My fingers danced on the steering wheel as I tried to compose my story in my head and with my fingers typing words on the wheel.

THE ASSISTANT MANAGING EDITOR at the newspaper, whom I got along with the best, was the toughest on reporters but the one they seemed to have the most respect for. When Chis edited their stories on deadline, he was keen to go back later and discuss with them all the changes he had made. His desk was not far from where I clipped stories for the newspaper's library. I listened in as much as I dared when Chis talked to the reporters about their writing.

Refine your lead until you have set a tone, then stick to that tone all the way through your story, Chis would tell reporters. Write your first paragraphs in your head on your way back from your assignment. By the time you sit down at your typewriter, you should be taking dictation from yourself. Engage the reader from the first word. Try to keep your lead paragraph under 30 words. Put the boring crap at the end. If you don't have a quote word-for-word, paraphrase. But paraphrase with care. Spell all names correctly. If you can't spell a name correctly, why should the reader believe anything else you write?

Chis had a habit of keeping copy he had edited in his desk drawer. Whenever I finished my clerk work early, I would go through his editing before Chis got to work to see if I could figure out the reasoning behind the changes he had made.

I had written a couple of short feature stories that I thought about asking Chis to read, but I chickened out. I didn't mind getting a C in a college course, but I feared the black pencil that Chis used when he edited copy. Every sentence had to count for something in a story Chis edited. Words were sacred to him and were always to be used with great care.

For an afternoon newspaper, the most hectic time was 10 o'clock in the morning. The Mid-South edition was put to bed, but the larger and more important Home edition would get all new stories and new page layouts. The Final edition had a smaller circulation and would mainly go to single-copy vendors and newspaper boxes.

Normally, only the front page and the jump pages would change for the Final.

I dropped off the roll of 35mm film with my one exposed frame to Twist 'n Shout in the photo lab and sat down at one of the typewriters used by the clerks. I took dictation from myself as I wrote my story. I realized that I didn't remember driving back to the newspaper from campus. I did vaguely recall that in order to save time, I had violated company rules and had parked my little car in one of the spaces reserved for staff cars. I would need to go down to move it when I turned in my story. I typed.

> *The stately pink sandstone buildings at Southwestern at Memphis stood in stark contrast today to a new color—the Army green of vehicles, tents and uniforms of the Tennessee National Guard that was bivouacked on campus.*

I had rewritten that lead paragraph dozens of times in my head on the way back to the newsroom. I couldn't remember the other versions. What I turned in was all that mattered. I put my story and its carbon copy in the city desk's wire basket forty minutes before the final-copy deadline. I kept an eye on it sitting in the basket as I pulled galley proofs out of pneumatic tubes and delivered them around the newsroom.

WAIT.

I rushed back, grabbed the story out of the basket and rolled the story into the closest typewriter. I typed at the top of the first page:

> *By Victor Vollmer*

The city desk would be responsible for adding the second line, "Special to The Press-Scimitar," the standard credit line that went to all writers who were not recognized members of the reporting staff.

"DAMN IT TO HELL," the managing editor screamed when I handed him the early proof of the Home edition's page one that I had retrieved from the composing room. He stormed out of his office and yelled across the newsroom to no one in particular and to everyone.

"For Christ's sake, people. Every soul in the entire universe knows Martin Luther King is dead," the managing editor said. He slammed the page proof down on the copydesk. "Put a second-day head and lead on the story for Christ's sake."

All conversations stopped when the managing editor was turning red and on a rampage. Only the wire machines and the pneumatic tubes made noise. Chis walked over to the copydesk with his page proof.

"I'll handle it," he calmly told the slot editor, the head of the copydesk. "Tell the composing room a new play headline and lead story are coming in five minutes."

The managing editor returned to his office and typewriters returned to their clacking.

One of my most important duties as a copy clerk was to go to the pressroom and pull the first ten newspapers of each edition off the press for delivery to the top editors in the newsroom. A loud horn would sound, and the thirty-year-old press that was two-stories tall would slowly crank up, like a train engine building up steam. Several hundred folded copies would slowly roll off as the inking on each page was adjusted by dozens of pressmen climbing around on the press scaffolding. The press foreman would nod to the clerk when it was okay to reach down and grab ten copies. This had to done in one clean motion to prevent jamming the press that eventually would ramp up to its running speed of 45,000 copies per hour. If a clerk ever jammed the press conveyor, he would not get the nod again from the press foreman until he was forgiven of his clumsy sin. My conveyor record was spotless.

As the press spit out its first unadjusted copies, I could read the new headline streamed across the top of page one in a bold 72-point font:

Attorney General Clark Confident

King's Assassin Will Be Captured

A good second-day headline like the managing editor wanted, but that was not the story in which I was most interested. Just before I was to go down to get the early copies, Chis had stopped me. "Nice lead on that campus story, Vic," he said. "I shortened it a little, but a good lead. And good on you for spelling 'bivouacked' correctly. Had to look that one up myself. It's a yeoman word, isn't it?"

I liked how Chis could get excited over a single word in the lead of story.

I scooped up the ten copies off the conveyor belt and started up the five flights of stairs. I had decided that the cranky elevator was too slow. At the first landing I stopped and flipped through the pages of the first section. At the bottom of a page with no advertisements was a two-column picture, credited only as a staff photo, and my story. I read the lead:

> The stately pink sandstone buildings at Southwestern at Memphis stood in stark contrast this morning to a new color bivouacked on campus – the green of the Tennessee National Guard.

Chis had taken out seven words to create a twenty-nine-word lead paragraph, but most everything else in the story was the way I had written it. Then the byline jumped out at me:

By Victor Vollmer
Press-Scimitar Staff Writer

I ran up the next four flights, two steps at a time. Someone on the city desk or copy desk had erred and identified me in the byline as a "staff writer." A mistake to be sure, but one that thrilled me.

MY SHIFT would be over in less than an hour. The city editor assigned me to monitor the police scanner while the desk editors took a quick lunch break in the company cafeteria. "Don't worry about routine fire-bombings and gang arrests, the city editor said, just make sure to come get us if they find the white Mustang or arrest somebody."

The scanner picked up the different radio signals from the city police, fire department and sheriff's department. The radio traffic was non-stop. Fires. Windows smashed. Looting. A white Mustang was stopped on Highway 51 North, but soon the 10-22 Code went out to disregard. In my three years working in the newsroom, I had learned most of the more than 100 "10-codes" used by law enforcement in their radio communications.

I opened a copy of the Home edition to my story again. I read it over and over to make sure nothing had been changed except the few words Chis had taken out of the lead paragraph. I checked the notebook again in my back pocket on the spelling of all the names.

Another copy clerk later in the day would clip all the local stories for the newspaper's library. I found a pair of scissors and snipped out my story and the photo I had taken. The "staff writer" designation had been a city desk mistake, but there it was for all the world to see and giving me a status of which I only dared dream.

I would be excited to show Phil—and Nellie—my first newspaper byline.

CHAPTER 6

BEING THE FASTEST TYPIST of all the copy clerks had its disadvantages. Just as my shift was ending, the city editor said he needed me to come in at my regular time at 4 o'clock in the morning on Saturday to type in more arrest records from the earlier riots. He said he wanted to publish as many as he could in the Saturday editions and that I should spend my entire four-hour shift typing in the arrests.

My glorious weekend-to-be with Phil was disappearing at every turn. I started to remind him that I had scheduled Saturday off, but I didn't dare do that considering the importance of the breaking news. Anyway, I needed the money. My small car got good mileage, but I would be using more gas than usual on the round trips to Nellie's.

Wire stories were being updated every half hour with news of more violence across the country. Washington and Chicago were the worst now. New York City had quieted down some after a rough Thursday night in Harlem. The civil unrest in Memphis, the site of the assassination, could be explained, but it seemed that most of the major urban areas in the country were under some form of lockdown. According to my high school history teacher, America's Revolutionary War in 1775 started when there was a "shot heard around the world." Almost 200 years later, the shot in Memphis seemed to me almost as loud. That would be a good phrase in a lead paragraph, I reasoned. I had to clinch my hands into fists so my fingers wouldn't start typing on something.

I considered going back to campus for another change of clothes to take to Nellie's, but I wanted to get back to Phil in Coldwater as quickly as possible.

National Guard trucks and jeeps were stationed throughout downtown as I made my way south out of the city on Highway 51 toward Coldwater. Shopkeepers had begun to put up sheets of plywood over their busted store windows. I watched as National Guardsmen and local law enforcement, sometimes working together, stopped and broke up any small group of young Black people walking together. They didn't bother so much with other people on the streets if they were white or old.

On the outskirts of Memphis, just before the Mississippi state line, Tennessee state troopers in two cars had stopped a Mustang, even though the car was more cream-colored than white, and the driver was a woman. I assumed all Mustangs that were even close to the color of white were being stopped.

At a small hardware store in Hernando, Mississippi, I stopped to see if I could find something to keep my canvas convertible top from flapping so badly. The only thing they had was black electrical tape and duct tape. I chose the electrical tape because it better matched the color of my top. I realized soon after I got going again that I had made a bad choice. The tape didn't stick to the canvas top uniformly. By the time I got to Arkabutla Road, the top of my car resembled the dark curls on Phil's head.

I was surprised to see a late-model Cadillac parked in front of Nellie's shack when I turned off the gravel road and onto the packed-dirt driveway. As I approached, I saw a nicely dressed Black man in a dark suit, white shirt and tie open a rear door of the car for his passenger, a blonde girl in a blue dress. The driver closed the rear door and efficiently slid into his front seat. The Cadillac took up most of the dirt drive, so I eased off into the grass. I waved to the inhabitants of the car as it passed but the windows were too dark to see if there was a response.

Nellie came out on her small porch as I parked. I had expected Phil to greet me but was disappointed when I didn't see her.

"Good noon day to you, Vic. We were wondering when you might be gettin' home."

"Where's Phil?" I asked.

"She's out walking the levee. Said she needed her some fresh air."

"I hope she doesn't get lost, all this country being new to her."

"No need to worry 'bout that girl," Nellie said. "I'd say that Miss Philomene can nigh take care of anything that comes her way." Nellie already had Phil sized up well.

Nellie opened the screen door. "Come on in and sit with me on the couch and tell me what all you been up to these last years. I can't get over looking at you as a grown man. It's proper you stopped me from calling you 'Little Man.' You not tall and slender like Mr. V, but you're broad and strong and got them good muscles for hitting and throwing that baseball."

I had never talked to Nellie about finding a document in the summer of 1959 that let me know that the man who married my mother was not my biological father. The document identified my father as "unknown." At the time, I reasoned that Nellie would have gotten on to me for snooping around in places that were supposed to be off limits to me. Now it seemed that this was the kind of information that Nellie might know without being told. I had started to write Phil about my dubious ancestry when I found out more about the divorce situation with my parents, but then I tore up the letter because it seemed so needlessly real to see everything written on paper. No good reason to bring up who was or was not my father now to Nellie. Water under the bridge. Maybe water over the levee was a better metaphor in Coldwater, Mississippi.

Nellie said that Phil had told her about my trip to Louisiana three years ago to spread Mr. Spiro's ashes in the Mississippi River. Nellie remembered meeting Mr. Spiro at our old house in midtown when he came by on his bicycle to leave me a note before he took off on one of his towboat trips up the river with a friend.

"I know you liked that old man with all his books that you met on Mr. Rat's newspaper route," she said. "I'm sorry that he had to leave this world, but we all have to and that's why we have to make the best of it whilst we be here."

Nellie would have understood Mr. Spiro's all-inclusive philosophy of life that he called the "Quartering of the Soul" and the four words that made for the examined life—student, servant, seller and seeker. Nellie lived that life with more composure and consistency than most, purposely keeping the four components in balance.

Our conversation eventually got around to my parents' divorce and Nellie offered that she could tell my mother and father were having their troubles when she was living with us in the house in midtown.

"I think Mrs. V wanted that new house out in East Memphis 'cause she thought it might change things around, but we each take our own houses with us wherever we go."

Those words sounded like something Mr. Spiro could hold forth on for an entire afternoon.

I explained why I liked working at the newspaper and that it was the one of the few places that felt like home after my parents split up.

"You know you could have come to see me anytime you wanted, Vic. I was missing you in the worst way, too. You don't know how many times I thought about asking Bernice to take me to the bus stop to go to Memphis, but everybody has to move on with their lives, especially young folks."

Nellie had put her basket of colored thread in her lap and was sorting it. I had never known her to have a conversation when she wasn't doing something with her hands, being it shelling peas, darning something or working on a needle story.

"I don't know why I didn't come see you," I said, "but that doesn't mean I didn't think about you."

Nellie continued to sort her thread, draping the different colors over the edge of her basket.

"Young boys are busy learning to be men," Nellie said. "You had your schooling to attend to and men things. I was proud to keep up with you through your letters that let me know you were okay. Sometimes I'd have Bernice read them two times to make sure I didn't miss nothing."

I had something I wanted to say but could not line up the words to ease into the subject, a talent that seemed to come easily to everybody else. The only thing to do was to blurt it out.

"I'm sorry you have to live in a house without a bathroom . . . I mean, one inside."

Nellie put her sewing basket to one side of the couch.

"Understand me now," she said as she locked her eyes on me. "I'm not having to. I want to live here because it suits me. Bernice and her family keep asking me to stay at her place, but she has her own life. I feel closer to where I know I belong out here, just like you say you feel like you belong at that newspaper. All God's animals have to decide where is the proper place to make their bed."

Nellie had given me a dispensation that I did not deserve, but I could not find the words to accept it. I had to change the subject.

"Was that the girl that you take care of that drove away in the Cadillac," I asked, already knowing the answer.

"That would be her. Pretty Miss Blythe. She brings a joy to me each day I'm with her," Nellie said. "I told her Daddy I didn't want anything for staying with her, but he opened me up an account in his bank in Tunica and keeps putting money in it. Bernice pays my light bill and takes a little money out and gives it to me when I need some, but I don't need much. The good Lord makes sure I want for nothing."

"How long have you helped out with B-B-Blythe?"

"I reckon I first kept her at her house when she was about 12. I still go over there some in bad weather 'cause I don't want her over here in this rickety house when it's storming, but I can't keep her away from those chickens." Nellie laughed. "She could feed and talk to those chickens all day, and I'm not too sure they don't understand her. Miss Blythe is a beautiful soul."

I wanted to ask Nellie about her own grandchildren that I didn't know anything about. Questions backed up in my head like newspapers on the press conveyor. I heard Phil open the back door and run water in the kitchen sink. She came into the front room with a bouquet of small blue wildflowers in a glass jar.

"We don't have these down in Louisiana," Phil said, "but they're blooming all over the levee."

"Them's called Forget-Me-Nots," Nellie said. "They'll be gone once this blackberry winter is done. They can't stand that levee heat without any shade. Good you picked 'em when you did."

"I thought they matched Miss Blythe's blue eyes," Phil said. "I'll give them to her tomorrow."

"Miss Blythe don't come of a Saturday unless her parents are out of town," Nellie said. "But they'll keep nicely for her if we keep 'em with fresh water."

Phil informed me that we needed to go to the grocery store, especially if I wanted more biscuits for supper. Bernice had come by before she went to work, but Phil said she told her that we would go get anything we needed when I got back from Memphis.

"We can just eat out," I said. Phil shot me one of her looks that told me I had said something out of order.

"Where's the best grocery store for baking soda and buttermilk?" Phil asked.

"I reckon down to Senatobia," Nellie said, "but I hate for y'all to go traipsing off on account of me."

"It's for me," I blurted out, trying to repair whatever damage I had done with Phil.

"Would they have slices of good country ham there?" Phil asked. "We don't eat much ham in Louisiana, but I have a taste for it."

"Sure should," Nellie said. "I got some crowder peas in the top of the icebox that we could have us a good mess of. And I can open a jar of chow-chow."

"We'll be back in a bit," Phil said. She was out the front screen door with more urgency than usual. The door slammed shut in my face before I could catch it.

THE TOWN OF SENATOBIA was five miles south on Highway 51 and Phil let me have it all the way there with a string of "did-you-knows."

Did I know that Nellie sent money orders every month to her family in Coldwater while she was working for my parents in Memphis?

Did I know that my parents always paid Nellie in cash—twenty dollars a week—so there would be no Social Security savings for her?

Did I know when Nellie moved back to Mississippi that she would walk behind the machines to pick "orphan cotton" for five cents a pound?

Did I know that for several years Nellie stood on her feet at the gin all day, picking field debris from the cotton?

Did I even know how old Nellie was?

Phil pelted me with questions until she finished me off with her *coup de grâce.*

"I think all you cared to know about Nellie Avant is how many of those good biscuits she can bake for you."

"B-b-but she got free room and b-b-board . . . and I saw my father give her extra m-m-money when she would sew b-b-buttons on his shirts," I said. "When he got new sh-sh-shirts, Nellie would take off the top b-b-buttons and sew them back on looser, the way he liked them."

My answers were spindly and pathetic, sounding worse the longer I heard myself on the defense. I kept going in the vacuum of Phil's silence.

"M-m-my mother was good to ask if she needed anything at the drugstore," I continued. "And she . . . m-m-my mother . . . would pay for it."

Phil rolled her eyes and accosted me with her silence once more.

"Nellie sure told you a lot while I was gone," I said, in a vain attempt to fend off the way Phil looked at me.

"Nellie didn't tell me squat," Phil said. "It was Bernice who told me when Nellie was out feeding the chickens with Blythe. And don't go blaming Bernice. I was the one asking questions about Nellie and her time in Memphis."

Changing the subject seemed to be my best tack.

"Nellie says she enjoys helping out with Bl-Bl-Blythe and that it's not even like work," I said, not knowing if my words were informational or just downright pitiful.

"And I *garantie* she enjoys it because she's a beautiful human being who has been given exactly nothing and expects exactly nothing," Phil said.

I pulled into the parking lot of a small grocery store that had prices for eggs, bologna and bread painted on the window in a crude typography. I faced Phil, feeling the need to try to somehow get the ball back over the net to her.

"So, what do you want me to do?" My response was clipped, curt and aggressive. Wrong question. Wrong tone. Wrong in every way imaginable. I could plan out my words for the sake of fluency, but the tone of my words could do me in.

"You do what you want, but stop calling Nellie Avant your 'best friend' and stop telling me how much you love her . . . 'cause what you loved is how much she could do for you . . . manboy."

Phil tried to slam her door when she got out, but the sliding windows made of scratched plastic and the lightweight door didn't make for good slamming. It barely ruffled the electrical tape on the ragged canvas top.

I had first heard Phil use the word "manboy" when she told me about a guy that she had once dated in New Orleans. I had asked her what the word meant. "Manboy" was a pejorative to the extreme. I had relished that she had referred to an old boyfriend in that tone. Now, it was coming back on me with a vengeance.

I sat alone in my car, alone with my "manboy" ways and feeling sorry for myself.

This was about the time the Friday night party would have started at the fraternity house, the festivities we had planned before the Old South Ball on Saturday night. And here I was in Senatobia, Mississippi, getting chewed out by the person I had vain-gloriously hoped was *my girl*. How did Phil and I manage to grow so far apart after our exhilarating meeting at the train station just twenty-four hours earlier?

Phil was in the checkout line with a small wire basket in her hand when I came into the grocery. I got behind her in line.

"I'll pay for this," I said.

"It's on me, Mister Vic," she said, imitating Nellie's name for me. She reached into the back pocket of her jeans. "You have to save your money to rent that Confederate uniform you were going to wear to THE BALL."

I had told Phil in a letter that some of my fraternity brothers were renting Confederate uniforms from a costume shop for the Old South Ball. I had thought about it myself but realized that I couldn't afford it. I had tried to explain once to Phil the reason I liked being in a fraternity and being a "brother." I was an only child. No brothers. I liked the fact that they chose me to join the fraternity instead of me choosing them. I didn't mind the ridiculous pledge rules and the hazing because it was the same for all the pledges. I stuttered when I had to repeat my ceremonial vows for full membership, but none of the brothers laughed. I liked to belong to something—in some official capacity—and know the secret handshake and the other fraternal markers. I knew the secret stuff wasn't important, but it made me feel special. Like I belonged somewhere. The last thing I bought of extravagance before being plunged into the poorhouse by my circumstances was a diamond and garnet-encrusted fraternity pin with our chapter designation engraved on the back. I rarely wore it, certainly not at work. I had considered asking Phil if I could "pin" her with it at some point like the other brothers did with their girlfriends, but that might draw blood now. Mine, most likely.

Phil's out-loud remark about the Confederate uniform embarrassed me. Others in the checkout line looked at me. Words piled up in my throat. Why did I have to pay for the sins of society? The sins of my father? The sins of my mother? Why did Phil have to treat me like I was a willing participant in all of that? I had invited her up for a pleasant weekend. Not an ass-chewing that had to do with generational customs.

I pushed ahead of Phil and through the customer stacking her groceries on the counter. I turned, stared at Phil and felt my foot slide off the brake.

"Go to hell," I said to Phil in a somewhat muffled voice. I had meant it as a shout, but I had trouble judging the loudness of my voice when I was on unsteady ground.

"What did you say?" Phil shot back. I reloaded. Just as my first utterance was not loud enough, my second was over the top.

"YOU GO TO HELL," I yelled at Phil. I turned and headed for the store's door.

A strange way to talk to the person whom I so hoped sometime during the weekend would be identified as *my girl*.

THE DRIVE to Senatobia had been a hurtful conversation. The drive back to Coldwater was more of a savage silence. The worry-haints were having their own festive Old South Ball in my head and in my gut.

I thought about apologizing for my loud words in the grocery store, but I felt like anything I said would make it worse. I had never cursed anyone, keeping myself in check with my foot on the brake even though I might be screaming on the inside. The only explanation I could come up with about my outburst was Mr. Spiro's mandate that love and hate were not opposites on the scale of emotions. They resided close to each other. I dared not bring-up that bit of Mr. Spiro's existential philosophy to Phil. She would find a way to slam it back at me with viciousness.

"We will not go into Nellie's house *furieux*," Phil said, as we pulled off the gravel road onto the dirt path. "We will not bring our *méchante* words into Nellie's house."

Phil's accent ramped up when she was angry.

"If you've *gris-gris* in mind, just keep yourself in the car." The French-Cajun words were some I had not heard before, but there was no doubt about their connotation.

I was depleted and confused.

"Look, Philomene, I know I've not done things right . . . but I feel like I'm alone now . . . without Nellie, without Mr. Spiro, without you. I just don't have my b—b—b—."

"Don't start that sputtering at me to make me feel sorry for you," Phil said. "I don't . . . "

". . . b-b-bearings," I finally said.

Did I actually stutter in order to gain sympathy? That was a new negative trait that Phil had assigned to me. A new one for the worry-haints to torture me with.

"I'm going on in," Phil said. "You stay out here until you get whatever kind of bearings you think you need." She exited the car with the sack of groceries.

Could I pretend that I had not cursed Phil? Did I try to stutter on purpose to make her feel sorry for me? It didn't feel like that, but I wasn't sure about anything as I sat in my car on a dirt driveway in Coldwater, Mississippi. Was being in a fraternity as bad as Phil made it sound? All I could think of that resembled a plan was Mr. Spiro's admonition to not fight the current.

PHIL AND NELLIE were chattering away in the kitchen when I walked in. Even Nellie couldn't tell that we had a fight.

I asked if I could help. No. As a peace offering, I asked if Phil would show me the levee before the darkness took over. No.

She suggested I take a walk by myself since supper wouldn't be ready for another half hour. I took her up on it; anything to get out of the house that the night before had felt so much like a safe haven. Phil could pretend for Nellie's sake that we had not had harsh words for each other. I did not have that ability. I was more than happy to take my leave.

The high levee started a few hundred yards from Nellie's shack. The top of the earthen dam was flat and forty-feet wide. The fresh breeze had been replaced by a hint of humidity that always seemed to be nearby in the mid-south. Probably wouldn't need a fire tonight, if I was even sleeping in the house. I had the idea that Phil might tell me to go back to Memphis and the fraternity house. Go spend the night with "your brothers," I could almost hear her say. Phil could turn a normal-sounding word like "brother" into something heinous.

I could make out the low-slung Arkabutla Dam and pumping station in the distance. Forget-Me-Nots were everywhere on the levee. I picked a handful as I walked, possibly to use as a peace offering.

My anger at Phil and my burst of harsh words surprised me. I would have never imagined I could have had those feelings for the person I so much wanted to be close to. The word "manboy" resonated with me. I didn't know how to gauge the word's ranking on Phil's negativity scale, but I suspected it ranked high. Chis would often coach young reporters to look for "holes" in their stories—in other words, major questions that were left unanswered. "That's a hole so big you could drive a truck through it," Chis would say. My relationship with Phil had a giant hole and I had no clue on how to fix it.

I started back to Nellie's shack. Coming down the side of the steep levee, I couldn't slow my steps in my leather-soled penny loafers, lost my balance and started sliding. My bum knee bent back under me as I fell. I knew I would be limping for a while. Phil, no doubt, would accuse me of wanting sympathy for my injury. When I got to my feet, my good pants were torn, covered with grass stains and streaks of levee dirt.

As I approached the shack, I looked at the wildflowers in my hand, which were now just a bunch of stalks with the delicate flowers in shreds. I cast the flowers aside, but Nellie's chickens apparently thought I was attempting to feed them. They came running and clucking to see what I had to offer. Then I saw the big white rooster coming from around the outhouse, straight at me in a run. It kicked wildly as it ran with wings outstretched. The bird launched itself at my legs. One of the rooster's spurs tore into my pants leg just above my shoe. I kicked at it with my good leg. It backed up and readied itself for another charge.

Nellie came out the back door, untying her apron and flapping it at the rooster. "You git from here," she yelled. "You best git or you'll wind up in that frying pan."

The rooster calmed down and began to shepherd its harem of chickens to the other side of the yard.

"That mean old cuss don't like menfolk coming 'round his hens," Nellie said. "I'll darn and wash those pants up for you. Good as new." I brushed myself off as best I could.

"You got that good timing," Nellie said, as we came in the back door. "We just about got supper on the table."

"That old rooster don't take to menfolk," she explained to Phil in the kitchen. I hoped Phil would see an opening to make a joke and let me know that she was going to ease up on me, but she let the opportunity pass without comment.

"Go wash up in my basin, Mister Vic," Nellie said. "We got this kitchen sink all full of pans." Nellie had always called my father "Mr. V," and now she had added "Mister" to Vic." I would have traded my $350 fraternity pin for a simple "Vic" without the "Mister."

Nellie's bedroom was not that much different than the room she lived in above the garage at our house—bed, chifforobe, chair and a table lamp with her Bible on it. My mother called it the "servant's quarters." I called it "Mam's room." I had always thought of it as a comfortable place, even though it was not insulated well and had only a bare light bulb hanging from the ceiling. There was no plumbing in the upstairs room. Nellie kept a wash basin on a small table with a chamber pot underneath, but she mostly used the downstairs half-bath in our house. When my parents were out of town, she spent the night in my room on a twin bed. It came to me then that I had never known Nellie to take a bath, although she was perpetually clean in her starched white uniform and smelled like Ivory soap.

I washed my hands in the basin. At the side of a mirror that was losing its finish was one of Nellie's needle stories tacked up on the wall—Moses and the burning bush. She told me when she was working on it in her upstairs room in Memphis that I would do well to study Moses because he had trouble saying his words like I did but that he didn't let that slow him down because he led his people for forty years to get them out of the wilderness and into the Promised Land.

Dr. Martin Luther King had said in his speech the night before he was assassinated that he had seen the Promised Land, just like Moses. I could see nothing from where I found myself. Near a dark levee in Coldwater, Mississippi, with the girl, no the woman, I so greatly cherished about ready to dump me overboard.

I INSISTED on helping Nellie do the dishes after supper. I thought I might be too upset to eat anything, but Nellie's cooking worked wonders for me. Phil said she would go in the front room and read the *Press-Scimitar* I had brought from work.

Helping wash dishes brought back pleasant memories from when Nellie lived with us and we would practice our "rounds" at the kitchen sink. I didn't feel much in the mood for silly rhymes, but then I remembered how good the carrying-on with Nellie always made me feel. As I had done so many times, I started a beat on the bottom of one of her pans with a spoon. Nellie joined in with a spoon clinking on her glass jar of bacon drippings. Maybe if Phil heard us carrying-on, she would think a little better of me. I could hope.

> *I do love*
> *Shortenin' bread*
> *I do love*
> *Shortenin' bread*
> *Mama love*
> *Shortenin' bread*
> *Papa love*
> *Shortenin' bread*
> *Everybody love.*
> *Shortenin' bread.*
>
> *Two little babies laying in the bed*
> *One play sick, the other'n play dead.*
>
> *I do love*
> *Shortenin' bread.*
> *I do love*
> *Shortenin' bread.*
>
> *Call for the doctor, doctor said*
> *Give them babies some shortenin' bread*
>
> *I do love*
> *Shortenin' bread*
> *I do love*
> *Shortenin' bread*

We continued the beat with our spoons. "What's that other verse?" I asked. Nellie picked it up.

> *Ever since my dog's been dead,*
> *Hogs been rootin' my tater bed.*

We both laughed like children on a playground. I spread my towel over the handle of the stove's oven to dry like I had seen Nellie do. She set the kitchen table with the clean dishes from the strainer.

"Can I ask you a question?" I asked.

"Always can," Nellie said and nodded.

"Did you t-t-teach me all those rhymes to try to help me with my st~ . . . with my talking?"

"Mainly just to have fun, I reckon" she said, "but I did pay a mind to how you said your words without any trouble when you rhymed words and sang."

"I thought so," I said.

"Didn't hurt nothing, did it?" Nellie asked.

"No, it didn't . . . and I enjoyed every m-m-minute of it," I said. "I think it may have helped me more than the speech th-therapy classes that my p-p-parents sent me to."

Nellie continued to set the table for breakfast.

"And I'll tell you s-s-something I've not told anybody," I continued. Anytime I know I have to speak in class or I have to make a telephone call and I start to get worried about my st-st-stuttering, I'll say some of the rhymes that you taught me to calm me down and it seems to help me."

Nellie smiled and nodded. "That's good," she said.

"Can I ask you something else?"

"My sakes, you're just full up with questions," Nellie said.

"I haven't seen you in so long and I've m-m-missed talking to you," I said.

"I've missed you, too," Nellie smiled. "Go on then."

"I read in the p-p-paper that Dr. King said on Wednesday night that he had seen the Promised Land and that he might not get there," I said. "Did you hear about him saying that?"

"I heard that on the radio," Nellie said. "He believes our peoples are wandering around in the wilderness like the Israelites and it's his job to lead us out like Moses. I'd say we need us a Moses for sure right about now, wouldn't you Mr. Vic?"

I could only nod. I had never had a discussion like this with Nellie—with anyone.

"Could you just call me 'Vic' without the 'Mister'?" I asked. "It would make me feel a lot b-b-better."

"If that's what you want," Nellie said. "I can't change that I'll always think of you as my 'Little Man,' but I'll call you anything that makes you happy."

Unlike most exchanges I managed to have with people, conversations with Nellie seemed to have a definitive outcome where something got accomplished.

Phil came into the kitchen with the newspaper open.

"I see you wrote something here about the National Guard being at that college of yours," Phil said.

I nodded. I had hoped she would see my story in the newspaper without me having to show her the clipping I had in my back pocket.

"It's my first b-b-byline." I tried to sound matter-of-fact with no emotion.

Nellie took off her apron and put it on the back of a kitchen chair. "Will you read it to me, Miss Philomene?" Nellie asked.

Phil looked at me and then spread the newspaper out on the kitchen table. Nellie sat down across from her and Phil read my story out loud. The words were mine. Ones I had written less than twelve hours ago. An added pleasure that I had not counted on was hearing Phil read the words.

"That's right good, Vic," Nellie said. "I remember walking by that pretty college over near the zoo. And you right. All them grand buildings is made of that pretty pink stone."

Phil closed the newspaper. "Will they pay you extra for that story?" Phil asked.

"I doubt it," I said, "since I was on the clock anyway."

"But they called you a staff writer," she said.

"It was a m-m-mistake in the rush of everything," I explained. "The editors ordered four extra p-p-pages in the edition and the copy desk was kind of shoveling stuff in."

"I like that story better than that cotton stuff you wrote," Phil said.

Any compliment from Phil was welcome in our current state. Phil and I moved over to the lumpy sofa. Nellie brought one of the kitchen chairs over. I decided it was time to test Phil's current state of mind.

"I n-n-need to be at work at four tomorrow morning to type some court stuff for the paper," I said to both Phil and Nellie. "Maybe I should drive b-b-back to Memphis tonight and sleep in my room at the fraternity house . . . so I won't wake anybody so early in the morning."

Phil halfway looked at me on the sofa.

"Paper here says that strict curfew is still in effect," Phil said. "You might get thrown in the hoosegow. If I were you, I'd just wait till morning to drive in."

Phil gave the answer I wanted to hear badly. Another night at Nellie's with Phil is exactly what I wanted a shot at even though I sensed we were far away from the good place I wanted us to be.

Nellie asked me what time I needed to leave Coldwater to get to work on time.

"A little after 3 a.m.," I said.

"You best get on to bed then. I'll have you some coffee and biscuits ready . . . and we have a few ham scraps left," Nellie said.

"Don't b-b-bother," I said. "I can get something at work."

"Not no bother," Nellie said. "You ain't changed so much that you won't eat a ham and biscuit, have you?" I looked at Phil and shook my head in the guilt that had been squarely laid upon me.

NELLIE PUT sticks of kindling in the wood stove along with pieces of cardboard she kept in a paper sack in the kitchen. She told me to add a few sticks of wood when the fire got going. That would heat up the room enough to get me through the night, she said. The warm breezes off the delta already had started coming back.

I took my loafers off and spread one of the quilts on the sofa over me. I turned on the radio to catch some news about what might be going on in Memphis, but then I cut the radio off when I heard Phil and Nellie mumbling in the back room. I strained with all my eavesdropping acumen to hear what they might be talking about, but all I could make out is that Phil was telling Nellie about her brothers and sisters and her life in Louisiana.

My bum knee had tightened up after my fall on the levee. It felt good to stretch it out on the sofa. I turned the radio back on to a low volume for more news but was asleep before I could add the first stick of wood to the stove.

Chapter 7

April 6, 1968
Saturday

SOMETHING tightened around my neck in the early morning brain fog I found in my head. I pulled at the tightening constrictor but could not open my sleep-ravaged eyes. Then the fuzzy image of a dull gray uniform with its upturned collar appeared in my mind's eye. A Confederate uniform made of wool on a blank-faced mannequin. I had tried on the uniform two years before in a costume shop with a group of fraternity brothers. I had just graduated from pledge to active status in the fraternal hierarchy.

I rubbed my throat where the non-existent collar raked against the skin of my neck .

Those once-harmless words—*Confederate uniform*—had sounded vulgar coming from Phil at the grocery store yesterday. I tossed and turned in the chill of the early Mississippi morning under Nellie's quilt.

The drowsiness, half dream and half consciousness, continued and I remembered the downtown hotel where we had booked the Old South Ball in the spring of my sophomore year. The management wouldn't let us display a Confederate battle flag behind the bandstand, explaining to the fraternity officers that it was against hotel policy. We agreed to take it down without much argument, not wanting to jeopardize our night of sanctioned partying that we had looked forward to all winter.

The special events manager told us in her professional tone and with pointed words that the hotel didn't approve of the fraternity's brothers coming to the party dressed in Confederate uniforms, but that she was not in a position to say what we should or should not wear. None of the brothers thought much about it. More of our thoughts were focused on how many kegs of beer would need to be ordered and what band we could afford.

Phil had the knack of putting a face—good or bad—on any word she chose. She bestowed the ugly mien on *Confederate*. Thankfully, I had not told her about the tradition of the president of the fraternity riding a horse over to the girls' dorms in a uniform with a sword and presenting flowers to the "Rose of the Old South Ball." That seemed a little over-the-top, even to me. The fraternity had voted two years before that if the president wanted to do it, he would have to foot the bill to rent the horse and sword himself, so the ritual had begun to die out.

The fuzziness in my brain complemented the fuzziness of my reasoning. My fraternity's Old South Ball was only a party, an excuse for everyone to drink beer, dance to a live band and have a good time. A chance to get away from textbooks. A reason for dates to put on fancy dresses. Ball gowns, they called them. Perhaps the custom was out-of-date and on the silly side, but no one in the fraternity ever talked about it as a political statement.

I continued to let my mind wander as I lay on the couch between uncomfortable sleep and wakefulness.

I recalled a recent day in the company lunchroom about the time the garbage worker strikes first started . I listened in as two long-time reporters from the other newspaper talked about how Memphis had escaped much of the racial violence that many cities in the South had experienced in the late 1950s and 1960s. Rosa Parks, a name I found intriguing, had refused to sit in the back of the bus in Montgomery, Alabama, in 1955. Little Rock, Arkansas, only 135 miles west of Memphis, had been ripped apart during federally mandated school desegregation in 1957. School desegregation had been going on in Memphis but without notable protest or extended violence.

One babbling reporter weighed in on the reason for the lack of racial conflict in Memphis, saying it had to do with the "plantation mentality" that was fostered in the city with the administration of the former mayor, E.H. "Boss" Crump. Boss Crump ruled with an iron fist and saw to it that no one got out of line, be the citizen Black or white. The other reporter, badly off-key, started singing: "Crump don't 'low no easy riders around here." He labeled the late mayor a "benevolent dictator" and was proud of his copy of a 1946 *Time* magazine with the white-haired Crump on the cover. Even though Crump died in 1954, the mayors since then had tried to manage the city the same way, but the power seemed to be slipping away with the growing strength of the labor unions and the Civil Rights Act of 1964. We were experiencing the "storm after the calm," was how one of the reporters put it. I was trying to study in the cafeteria over coffee after my shift was over but eavesdropping on plain-spoken reporters seemed more relevant than any college history class.

I wondered what a Black person would have made of that conversation. Was there a "calm" or had the pot been boiling on a low heat that white people did not notice? I wanted to ask the reporters their opinion, but that would have exposed my eavesdropping.

I must have gone back to sleep because my next sensation was that I smelled coffee brewing. I slipped on my shoes in the darkness and went to the kitchen, illuminated only by a single light bulb hanging from a twisted wire in the middle of the room.

"Mornin' to you," Nellie said. "That coffee be dripped soon." Phil remained in Nellie's bedroom in the back of the house with the door closed. At least, I hoped she was still in there.

Nellie quietly hummed one of her church hymns as she busied about the stove. Her movements around the kitchen had always mesmerized me, handling pots with both hands and adjusting the flame of the gas stove like she was setting the hands of a clock. If she had ever spilled a drop of anything, I never saw it. When my mother cooked in the kitchen in our new house, pots banged, crashed and spilled their contents. Nellie managed everything with a quiet and dignified grace that I loved watching.

"I need to go out . . . out back," I said.

"Don't worry 'bout that ol' rooster bothering you," Nellie said. "You're up even 'fore that old cock this morning."

When I came back in the kitchen, I wanted to ask Nellie questions about "plantation mentality" and if "her people," as she called them, actually were "calm" before Dr. King was killed, but the questions didn't make sense as I tried to line them up in my head. Something else came out of my mouth.

"I like your house," I said, wondering how I happened upon that dime-store statement.

"Suits me just fine, too, Vic," Nellie answered. I wondered if she found it as strange calling me "Vic" as I did calling her "Nellie." Then I remembered her admonition that no matter what names are used, *we always are who we were.*

PHIL CAME into the front room while I was drinking my first coffee. I could only stare. Instead of jeans, she had on a simple purple dress with small flowers printed on it and a pair of black shoes with low heels that I had never seen before. The shoes made a different sound than her tennis shoes on the wood floor. The dress was not tight like her jeans, but it pinched in on her waist at the most appropriate spot. Her curls were combed into abeyance, or at least a valiant attempt had been made.

"Don't you look nice, Miss Philomene," Nellie said. I nodded and continued to stare, never having seen Phil in a dress before.

"I thought I'd better wear this thing since I went to the trouble of bringing it," Phil said, then looked at me. "I'm going to the newspaper office with you this morning."

"It's early . . . but that's f-f-fine," I said, trying to hide my surprise. No need to get into another argument, which I would be certain to lose. I pictured Phil at the now-cancelled Old South Ball in her simple print dress. She would have been the show, even with all the other dates in their frilly ball gowns. Phil brought her own space and universe along with her wherever she went. I warned myself not to look too hard at her. The word was not "hard." Longingly.

Nellie took four fluffy biscuits out of the oven, sliced them open and stuck in slices of country ham that had been sizzling in the skillet. She poured Phil a cup of coffee and filled mine.

"Mind if I spoon a little of your *mélasse* in my coffee?" Phil asked Nellie.

"Go right ahead, Miss Philomene. You put in as much kick as you want," Nellie said. I thought about making a joke about the strength of Louisiana coffee, but I was still trying to come to some sense of where I stood with Phil. Her use of French for "molasses" told me she was still not in a mood to be trifled with.

"You two be mindful up there in Memphis today," Nellie said. "Won't surprise me none if they is still out on the streets, still upset and wanting to fight about what was done to Dr. King."
I nodded.

"What good do they think that settin' fires and bustin' windows is gonna do?" Nellie continued, shaking her head. "All they is doin' is hurtin' their own. Dr. King would be upset at all the foolish violence and how the people is acting, even after what was done to him."

"I believe in non-violence too, as far as it goes," Phil said, "but sometimes you have to get a body's *attention*." Phil's French pronunciation of the noun gave it unmistakable weight and resonance

I looked at my wristwatch as I took the last bite of my ham and biscuit that seemed to flush away months of eating old cheese and stale crackers.

"We probably need to get on the road," I announced.

"Y'all take these two biscuits with you," Nellie said. "I'll wrap them up in some waxed paper."

Phil grabbed the plate and put it back in the warm oven. I took her cue.

"I can't eat another bite," I said, trying to convince myself of that statement.

"Neither can I, sure," Phil added. "My mama used to call these cathead biscuits."

"I heard them called that, but I never did," Nellie said. "All I could think of was eating the head off a cat, and I never been that hungry. They'll be here for you when y'all gits back."

"You have them for your lunch, Nellie," Phil said. "We'll probably be gone most of the day. I want you to tell me tonight how many eggs you get this morning. Miss Blythe will want to know too."

"I'll let her know the count when she comes on Monday," Nellie said. "That girl can tell you back to the month how many eggs her chickens laid. She is something special, I tell you."

Phil gave Nellie a goodbye hug.

I wanted to join in the hug, too, but my head was caught up in the swirling anticipation of what the day with Phil going to the newsroom with me was going to bring and the guilty knowledge that I would have loved to have taken one of those extra ham and biscuits with me.

Phil had her small bag with the helicopter logo on it when she came to the car. She put the bag in the trunk even though I assumed we would be back at Nellie's to spend the night. I looked at her stow the bag away but didn't say anything. We got in the car.

"None of your busyness, sure," Phil said calmly as she settled in her seat.

"What's none of my b-b-business?"

"The reason I'm bringing my bag with me."

"Okay. Fine. It's n-n-none of my business."

In addition to running down swamp rabbits, piloting fishing boats in the Gulf and saving me from drowning in the river, Philomene Moreau also was an accomplished reader of my mind.

SILENCE ENVELOPED the car even though the disheveled convertible top with its pitiful tape job flapped in the wind violently as I drove toward Memphis.

I could tell I was going to have to do the talking to try to manage the uncomfortable silence. Why did Phil choose to come with me for the day if she was so upset with me? I couldn't make sense of it.

It finally came to me to share one of Mr. Spiro's best stories that he had told me the year before he died. We were sitting on a bench in Tom Lee Park on the Memphis riverfront one weekend soon after I'd received my driver's license. I remembered his words well even though it had been almost five years since I had heard my late friend tell his story in his special way.

Tom Lee, a Black man, was out on the Mississippi River in his small boat when a sternwheeler carrying a large group of Memphis dignitaries on a social outing capsized in the river. Lee, who worked for a company that maintained the riverbanks around Memphis, saw what was happening far out in the swift current and took quick action. Over the next four hours, Tom Lee rescued thirty-two people from the roiling river. He could pack only eight people into his small boat, so he had to make four trips into the dangerous current. He ferried men, women and children he pulled from the river to the closest sandbars. Larger boats came to the rescue of other passengers, but Tom Lee was responsible for the most saved lives that afternoon. In the end, twenty-three people from the sternwheeler drowned. Continuing to risk his life, he searched the river well into the night as he recovered bodies. Tom Lee was declared a hero, even going to Washington, D.C., to shake the hand of President Coolidge. The small park on the river and an obelisk were dedicated in his memory.

Mr. Spiro had told me the story like he was there, but it had happened in 1925. He said the sign at the park identified Tom Lee as a "worthy Negro," a sad description for a true hero.

Mr. Spiro ended his stories with words that kept ringing in my ears. I tried to repeat them verbatim for Phil in Mr. Spiro's resonating voice without any stutters: "It turns out Mr. Lee's heroic endeavor was appropriately magnified when it was discovered that he was forty years of age but had never learned to swim."

Phil glanced at me. I knew Phil would appreciate the story because it had to do with the river, but I had an important update to Mr. Spiro's tale; another sobering ending to the story for the time and place the city found itself.

"I've been reading old newspapers in the library in my sp-sp-spare time . . . and found out that Tom Lee spent the last twenty years of his life as a garbage man, making twenty cents an hour," I said, offering the best inflection with the least amount of stuttering on my carefully chosen words. "Today they're called s-s-sanitation workers, but they were called 'garbage men' when they made twenty cents an hour . . . and that was not all that long ago."

I sneaked a look at Phil for some reaction. She stared straight ahead, but I could tell that she had been listening to my story. There were more river tales I considered sharing, but I thought it best to let the next words be hers. I waited. With her right hand out the window, she fiddled with the black tape on my car's top.

"You know that story you talked about where Dr. King said that he had been to the mountaintop and had seen the Promised Land," she said.

I nodded.

"Back when we were outrunning Hurricane Betsy, do you remember telling me something your Mr. Spiro said about intellect and intuition and how it was best if they worked together?"

I nodded again, amazed that Phil had remembered my fumbling explanation of something that must have seemed frightfully esoteric coming out of my stuttering mouth. Mr. Spiro's theory purported that to make proper decisions, we had to use both the intelligence of fact and the existential worth of intuition.

"I read that story of Dr. King's speech in the Friday newspaper you brought us. He said that he might not get to the Promised Land with his people. So, do you think he had the *intuition* that he was going to die?"

Phil pronounced "intuition" in French, but it was the same word.

"Maybe so," I said. "But I'm not so s-s-sure he thought it would be the next day."

I wanted to keep the conversation going.

"Both Memphis newspapers offered twenty-five-thousand-dollar rewards to anybody who could help find his killer," I said.

"From what I can tell, your newspaper didn't think that Dr. King should be stirring up trouble in Memphis," Phil said. Both Memphis newspapers had written long editorials against the strike since the first protest march on March 28, but I had no idea how Phil knew any of this.

"I don't think that Dr. King m-m-meant for things to get out of hand," I said. "He was probably just as surprised as anyone . . . and came here m-m-mainly to calm things down." Phil nodded her agreement at my assessment.

Our short but non-combative conversation helped calm me. I could feel my breaths coming easier. In the early morning emptiness, I didn't see any problem with switching over to Highway 61 and taking Riverfront Drive into downtown Memphis. I pointed out Tom Lee Park to Phil as we passed and turned over a question in my mind that seemed suitable for the situation.

"I wonder what Tom Lee would think about all this . . . all the v-v-violence that's going on now?"

Phil looked out to the river as she spoke.

"He'd probably say that Ol' Man River just keeps on rolling . . . and maybe that things haven't changed as much as they should have in the last hundred years."

A SPOT in the newspaper's employee parking lot was easy to find at 4 o'clock in the morning.

"This is the first time I've seen you in a d-d-dress," I said, when I turned off the ignition. "You look nice."

Phil didn't handle compliments well.

"Well, I'll have to say you look like you been sleeping a full week in those clothes you have on," she said. "After you finish your typing for the newspaper, you might ought to see if you can find some fresh clothes you can change into. After all, you don't want your 'Cajun queen' to be seen with a rumpled-up frat boy, now do you?"

Phil's way of speaking that I had longed to hear for three years could cut both ways—approbative and pejorative—two words that my enthusiastic rhetoric teacher loved to use. I only knew I felt about as ragged as my convertible top when Phil chose to come at me with words knotted up with her anger.

"I'm sorry, Vic," she said. "I need to stop picking fights with you, but I think after you get finished with your work that we need to go somewhere and have a sit-down talk. Both of us should have realized that it's hard to pick up where we left off after three years . . . even with all your good letters."

I nodded, grateful for the positive critique of my words to her on paper, but worried about what she might have in mind for our impending discussion. Would I get another dressing-down about being a *manboy*? Would she blame me for the "plantation mentality" of my city?

"You've changed . . . and maybe I have too," Phil said. "We just need to slow down and have us a serious talk . . . *coeur à coeur*—heart to heart."

Questions piled up inside me as we sat in the car. Had I changed so much that Phil no longer liked to be with me? Did we have any chance of getting back to where I thought we once were while I was writing her letters as her pretend boyfriend? Did we have any kind of future together?

When questions from the worry-haints overwhelmed me, my tendency was to shut down. Phil talked through her emotions while I let mine gnaw at my bones from the inside.

"We'd better get on up to the newsroom for you to get started," Phil finally said after we had sat silently in the car for a while. "No need to leave for work so early in the morning just to be late. I'll read the papers while you're working. They won't kick me out, will they?"

"I'll find you a good spot to read in the morgue," I said.

"I don't like that word," she shot back. "*Morgue.*" The French pronunciation had a sinister sound to it.

"Right," I said. "I don't really l-l-like it either. It's l-l-library from now on."

To my surprise, I was looking forward to the mindless typing of arrest reports that lay ahead of me. Anything to escape the worry-haints tugging at me as I wondered what Phil wanted to talk about—heart to heart.

THE CITY DESK night editors were still at their desks when we walked into the fifth-floor newsroom. They would soon hand off their stories and notes to the day-side crew who came in at 5 a.m. The copy desk editors, who designed the pages, wrote headlines and edited the copy a final time, had all come in early for their shifts since the managing editor took the day's paper up again by four pages. Two other copy clerks were on duty, one sorting mail and the other ripping wire copy for the wire editors on the copydesk.

The library was always open even though the librarians didn't come in until 8 in the morning. I found Phil a copy of Saturday morning's newspaper. The bold headline read:

Rioters Ravage Major Cities

The first paragraphs of the wire story said federal troops in full combat gear had surrounded the Capitol and White House for protection. A machine-gun post had been set up near the Capitol building to protect it from the gathering mob, but the protest had been peaceful. No shots had been fired and no one was hurt.

There didn't seem to be much new on the local front. The search had broadened throughout the South for the man driving a white Mustang who had checked into a rooming house across the street from the Lorraine Motel. The man had registered as "John Willard." The rooming house—our cop reporters called them "hot-pillow motels"—was owned by a Bessie Brewer and her husband, Frank, according to the newspaper.

"He was a clean, neat man," Mr. Brewer was quoted as saying. "I showed him Room 8 at ten dollars a week with a kitchenette, but he said he only wanted a sleeping room. I showed him Room 5 and he said, 'This'll be fine.' "

The story went on to say that Room 4 was rented by a Willie Anchutz, a local man who worked for a moving and storage company. "Mr. Anchutz saw the killer immediately after the shooting, running downstairs carrying something that was long and wrapped up in a blanket," Brewer told the reporter.

I passed by the city desk to hear the lead police reporter and the city editor arguing over a story the reporter had just turned in after apparently working all night on it. The reporter had quoted one of his confidential police sources as saying that Dr. King had been killed by a .30-06 bullet known as a "dumdum," the kind that hunters used on big game. The reporter had quoted another unnamed source in his story that a palm print was discovered on the rifle that had been found outside the rooming house. The city editor told the reporter that the unnamed sources would have to be identified. The reporter, the newspaper's resident expert on all things having to do with firearms, vowed to go over the city editor's head to the managing editor. I busied myself around the city desk to hear the outcome of the argument. The managing editor came to the city desk and, after some thought, ruled it okay to run the story without identifying the sources by name.

"Just make it 'a source close to the investigation,'" the managing editor said.

"Do you know the source?" the city editor asked his boss.

"Just do like I said and don't ask questions," the managing editor said. The newsroom hierarchy was set in stone.
COPIES OF COURT DOCUMENTS and arrest reports filled my mailbox slot to overflowing. I wasn't sure how long it would take me to transcribe them, even though I was familiar with the format. I wanted to try to finish in four hours so Phil and I would have almost the entire day to ourselves, even though there would be no fraternity party and I didn't have the first idea of how we were going to spend the day.

I typed the first arrest report:

> *Clarence T. Ball, 26, Negro, 1199 Lauderdale; city and state charges of carrying a pistol and threatening breach of the peace; bond set at $750, continued until April 24.*

This was the standard form for typing: name, age, race, address, charge, bond. The only exception was that if a white person was charged, race would be omitted with the reader left to assume that the person was white. The courts were bad about misspelling street names, and it was up to me to catch the mistakes. I prided myself on knowing how to spell most of the street names in Memphis.

This kind of typing put me into a trance, but one that I could count on to serve me well. Of the hundreds, maybe thousands of arrest reports I had typed over the years, a correction had never come back on me. The city desk kept detailed records of all corrections. If you got caught in more than three mistakes, you would have to go and get blessed out by the managing editor.

After every three pages completed, I would walk my copy over to the city desk and place it in the basket along with the carbon. I peeked in the library at Phil with newspapers spread out around her. She looked up.

"How's it going with the typing," she asked.

"Not bad. I think we have a sh-sh-shot at getting out of here on time," I said.
"Don't hurry on account of me," she said. "Where will I find us some coffee in this building?"

I told her that the lunchroom on the third floor should be open.

"I can go get it if you want," I said.

She started putting the sections of the newspapers back together.

"You just keep those fingers flying," she said. "I'll be back quick, sure."

As I rolled another sheet of paper and carbon into the typewriter, I noticed an animated conversation going on between the managing editor and Chis, the editor who had edited my campus story on Friday. The two were going at it red-faced in the managing editor's office. Reporters peeked up from their typewriters every now and then to take in the war of words. Even though I couldn't hear all the exchanges, I had a good idea what the argument was about. The glass that made up the top of the office walls rattled when the managing editor slammed the door behind Chis. I gladly concentrated on my typing.

"Imbecilic. Imbecilic. Imbecilic," Chis muttered as he sat down at his desk. He had been trying to quit smoking, but he rifled through his desk and came up with an old pack of cigarettes. He walked over to my typing station.

"You got a light, Vic?" He answered his own question. "Of course, you don't. You don't smoke. And good for you."

I went to the desk where the clerks did maintenance on typewriters. A lighter was kept in the drawer that I used to heat up a tool that cleaned the ink out of badly clogged typewriter keys.

I handed Chis the lighter. "Anything I can help with?" I asked.

He looked at me and smiled. "Can you rid this newsroom of imbeciles?" he asked.

"My sh-sh-shift is only four hours." I hoped he had gotten my attempt at a joke.

Chis smiled and offered a truncated laugh. "Thanks, Vic," he said. "I needed that."

He sat down at his desk, put the old pack of cigarettes back in his middle drawer and pulled out a black editing pencil.

"I have this long-running argument with the powers that be here that we have to stop this nonsense of putting race in crime stories and listings," he said. "It makes no sense. It's blatant racism at its very core. The only time race should be used in a story or listing is when a suspect—white or Black—is being actively sought and it's part of a physical description along with height, weight and clothing."

"I'm typing a b-b-bunch of arrest reports now and race is in all of them," I said.

"That's exactly what I'm talking about. I've protested until I'm blue in the face," he said.

I had typed "Negro" thousands of times over the years and had never thought about it. The word was simply part of a form that someone in the police station had filled out.

"You might s-s-say that an address is a better identification anyway," I offered.

"You're damn right," Chis said. "When things quieten down, if they ever do, I'm going to start a newsroom petition to get the policy changed and stop this racist foolishness. Will you sign it?"

"Sure," I nodded. "N-n-not that it will mean much me signing anything."

"There's power in numbers, Vic. You'll be seeing that power on the streets of Memphis this week . . . and, I hate to say it, it's about time," Chis said.

"I guess I b-b-better get back to my typing," I said.

"That'll wait," Chis said, sharpening his pencil with a pen knife from his drawer. "I want you to look around the newsroom and tell me what kind of people you see."

I didn't know what he was getting at.

"You m-m-mean, reporters and editors," I said.

"Okay, so tell me what you don't see," Chis said.

"Oh," I said, embarrassed that it took me so long to understand his point. "Ev-ev-everybody here is white."

Chis smiled. "Exactly," he said. "The minority population in Memphis is close to forty percent now. It makes no sense that this newsroom is so lily white . . . if we are to be a newspaper for all the people."

Chis looked at one of the many wall clocks that held sentry in the newsroom.

"You'd better get back to typing your crime reports," Chis said. "We'll have to get the next edition out before we solve all the world's problems."

He pulled out a fresh set of galley proofs to attack with his editing pencil.

Typing "Negro" took one stroke from my right hand, three from the left and another one from the right. After the conversation with Chis, typing the word felt odd. *Wrong. Violate. Contravened. Infructuous.* The inflated synonyms from my tattered *Roget's Thesarus* that I kept in in the trunk of my car came at me in waves.

For the first time, I felt my fingers imitating a stutter as I typed "Negro."

PHIL HAD ONLY one Styrofoam cup of coffee when she got back to the fifth floor.

"Where's yours?" I asked.

"I was chatting with some fellas out on the dock and drank mine," she said. "I hope yours is not cold."

"The dock?"

"You know, the loading dock, where the paper bundles are put on the trucks," she explained.

I had never set foot on the loading dock in all my time at the publishing company. If I gave Phil enough time, she would be operating a Linotype machine in the composing room or fine-tuning the ink valves on the press.

"There's some interesting guys out there working on the docks," Phil said. "One of them told me a story about a book that was interesting."

"What kind of b-b-book?"

"It's a long story. I'll tell you later," she said. "You best get on with that typing so we can get out of here and get on with our getting."

Phil seemed in a better mood. My typing sped up substantially.

I FINISHED the 250 or so arrest reports that I had pulled from my mailbox with five minutes to spare on my four-hour shift.

Instead of announcing to the city desk I had finished and risking more assignments, I slipped the final sheets of copy in the basket and motioned for Phil to head for the elevator. At last. We had almost an entire day to ourselves. A walk along the river. A visit to my old neighborhood where I had subbed on Rat's paper route almost ten years ago. The only problem is that the city was still mostly shutdown with law enforcement and the National Guard milling about everywhere.

We reached the car. Instead of coming up with a grandiose plan for the day, I couldn't get my mind off the newly distasteful feeling of typing the arrest reports, something I had done countless times.

"Any th-th-thoughts about what you would like to do today?" I asked.

"First thing . . . how 'bout we get you some clean clothes and maybe a shower," Phil said. "I'm afraid you might start to smell like the bait-well on Daddy's boat."

She smiled. A smile which I needed in the worst way. Also, her assessment of my physical state was not far from the truth. Memphis humidity could compete with the heat of South Louisiana any day.

"If the guard I know is b-b-back at the gate, I think he'll let us through and I can s-s-slip in the fraternity house to get some clothes," I said. "Only thing is, I'll have to go to the gym to shower and that will leave you in the car b-b-by yourself."

"Why can't I go in the fraternity house?" she asked.

"Well, there m-m-might be some b-b-brothers . . . ."

Phil could tell when my stutter was accentuated by pressures not fully related to my speech impediment. She put her hand to her chest, but I grabbed it playfully.

"Don't do your southern b-b-belle swoon again," I said. "I'm well aware you can take care of yourself."

She put a hand on top of mine on the gearshift. I had seen those hands gut and fillet a 200-pound tuna and then delicately build a mud pack to close up an open wound when I gashed my head tumbling out of her boat into the river. No manicures. No polish. No rings on those hands. The strong and capable hand of Philomene Moreau felt so right resting on the top of mine.

THE FRIENDLY GUARD with his clipboard came out of his shack at the entrance gate to the college. No dutiful rent-a-cop this time. Luck was with us. I explained that Phil was my older sister who was visiting and that I had to get something from the fraternity house and then we would be on our way. Lying seemed to be coming more natural to me.

As we drove to the lot near the fraternity houses, Phil surprised me.

"Me, I'd rather be your girlfriend than your sister any day, sure," she said.

A moment's hesitation and then I shot back: "So, how do we make that happen?"

My words surprised me. Was I finally learning how to take my foot off the brake?

"First thing is to get some of that stink off you," Phil said. Deflecting my serious questions was another trick she had mastered. I longed to know the answer to my question, but no answer was coming.

I opened the trunk to remind myself what clothes I had stored there and saw the newspaper's camera I had used the day before. I had forgotten to turn it in, but it would be safe there. And there was Phil's bag that she had mysteriously placed in the trunk that morning. Why?

College rules stated co-eds were not allowed in fraternity houses except during sanctioned events registered with the college's activities board. The rules also mandated that alcohol was not allowed in fraternity houses. Both edicts were regularly flaunted, but there was no back way into the house, so we would need to slip in the front through the large arched door. I had no idea who, if anyone, would be in the frat house at eight-thirty on a Saturday morning during a curfew.

My worst fears were realized. I opened the door and heard stereo music and laughter coming from the billiard room in the back of the house. The stairs up to my tiny attic cubicle were in the game room. Nothing to do but forge on.

The wolf whistles and not-unexpected cat calls began the moment Phil and I stepped through the open double doors.

"Whoa, mama."

"Lookie, lookie, here comes cookie."

"Be still my heart."

One of the more musical brothers, who was known to do a respectable Frankie Valli, started a boozy "Can't Take My Eyes Off You," off-key and just enough to be comedic.

The brothers put their pool cues on the table. Game over. Those sitting in the leather chairs stood. Their attire ranged from sweatpants to shirts wrinkled worse than mine. By the number of half-empty beer cups on the stairs and window ledges, the party had been going on most of the night. No need to let a rented keg go to waste, the brothers evidently had decided.

"Okay, knock it off," I said. "This is Phil . . . Philomene . . . my fr-fr-friend from Louisiana I've been telling you about."

"*Comment allez-vous, mes chères,*" Phil said with her infectious smile, a wave of her hand and a half bow.

A photo of the group in that instant would have captured ten hungover and wobbly fraternity brothers with their mouths agape. A second semester pledge we had nick-named "Jersey" had backed up to sit on an arm of one of the leather chairs and immediately slid off onto the floor. Paul, a member of the varsity basketball team, went to put his hand on the wall to steady himself and hit the side of the cue rack, sending all the cues not in use crashing to the floor. Phil's laughter and smile served to bring some oxygen back in the room.

I looked at Phil as if to give her the okay. She took it and ran with it.

"You are an *impressionnant* bunch, sure," Phil announced. She looked at Paul. "Does your *mama* know where you been last night?" Phil's satirical "mama" was in two distinct Cajun syllables with the accent on the last.

Half the heads nodded "yes" and the other half shook "no." This was too much fun, but we needed to get on with our get.

"I need some cl-cl-clothes and razor out of my room and then go to shower," I told the brothers, who still had their eyes fixed on their visitor. "Phil is going to stay here while I'm sh-sh-sh . . . at the gym."

The pledge who had slipped off the chair needed to regain some of his cool after his spill on the floor.

"Aren't you afraid to leave Philomene here with all these handsome brothers here?" he said.

"Afraid, sure . . . afraid for you," I said. For once, I had gotten the pause and the timing right for my joke.

I took Phil by the hand.

I didn't dare look, but I could feel the brothers watch Phil follow me up the stairs. *My girl.* No, *my woman.* If I had written it in a movie script, Phil's introduction to my fraternity brothers could not have gone better.

FEW STUDENTS showered at the gym in the morning besides me, especially on a Saturday. The water from the boilers took forever to become even lukewarm. I quickly shaved and put on a clean polo shirt and khaki pants. I thought I would feel anxious leaving Phil at the house, but she had me dead to rights. I did want to show her off, and the best way to do that was to let Phil be Phil. I would only have to share her for half an hour or so. I was beginning to understand that I didn't have to have a plan set in stone for Phil. Let things happen. Let go. Don't fight the current.

National Guard vehicles, mostly six-wheeled troop carriers, rumbled through the narrow campus streets as I walked back to the fraternity house. Large tents had sprung up in the open fields behind the gym. The portable kitchens on wheels and attached to jeeps had served breakfast and looked as if they were being readied for lunch. I halfway thought about proposing to the city editor a follow-up story on the Guard presence in the city but then decided that this reporter was off the clock for two more days until . . . until . . . I hated to think about it . . . until Phil caught the City of New Orleans early on Monday morning back to Louisiana.

The cruel words, the shaky moments that Phil and I had experienced the first two days were not fun, but they were real, and I had come to realize that it could only be that way with Phil. I was learning more explicitly that she could not abide anything but the truth. Pretense of any kind was a poison to her. I liked to think I had that same notion, but she wore it more naturally than I.

When I opened the front door to a quieter fraternity house, I heard cue balls colliding in the game room, but the chatter was missing. Phil was running the table on one of the brothers as the rest of the group watched.

"I hope you used soap, Sporty Boy." Phil winked at me as I came into the room. I was proud she took the opportunity to slip in her special "Sporty Boy" for the brothers to hear.

"Has Phil already taken all your weekly allowances?" I asked the strangely quiet group. "I forgot to mention that they play a lot of p-p-pool down in South Louisiana."

"We just played a few friendly games of nine-ball, but funny thing is that I'm still playing, and no one has taken the cue away from me," Phil said.

Two or three of the brothers had left the house and the rest were noticeably subdued. Someone had moved the keg into the chapter room and cleaned up all the empty plastic cups that had littered the windowsills. I watched Phil make a long bank shot on the nine-ball to end the game.

"I think I may have ruined the party for your friends while you were showering," Phil said. I started to laugh and then realized that she was serious.

"How's that?"

I was sorry I had asked.

"I told them I didn't think too much of their big Confederate flag hanging in that other room there and they should take it down," Phil said. She walked over to put her cue in its rack on the wall. "They said it was just a 'prop' and didn't mean anything."

One of the fraternity officers spoke.

"We're supposed to keep it hanging in the chapter room. That's all. It's a part of the heritage of the Order. It doesn't hurt anything . . . or anybody."

Phil's turn.

"What you know is that it doesn't hurt you boys. How 'bout we go over to the Jewish fraternity house and hang us a big Nazi flag there. It's just a flag. It can't hurt nobody Or maybe we invite the Black fraternity to come over here and drape their flag around your painting of Robert E. Lee sitting on his horse. Can't hurt anything. It's just an old flag."

I had no clue Phil knew anything about the Greek fraternal system and that Jewish and Black fraternities even existed.

The fraternity officer shot back at Phil. "There's none of those houses on campus," he said, completely missing her point. "We'll . . . why you think that might be, *frère?*" Phil said, in her sarcastic best.

Phil dug in the leather pockets of the pool table and pulled out the white cue ball and the black eight ball. She slammed them on the middle of the table.

"Look at your two pool balls sitting there," she said. "Show me which one rolls better. Tell me which one is more perfectly round. Show me which one banks better. You can't. Only difference between them is one is black and one is white."

She looked at me and shrugged her shoulders. I looked at my dumfounded fraternity brothers. They shook their heads, but not a one had a challenge for Phil.

"My *couillon* mouth has over run my good sense again," Phil said to me. An apology, it was not. "I think it's because I just spent two days with the most wonderful human being on God's earth . . . and she has no flag to fly."

Phil couldn't stop and her seriousness filled the room.

"And come to think of it, mister fraternity boys, I don't have anything to fly either, so if you happen to run across some kind of a flag for a loudmouth South Louisiana coonass, let me know."

Phil took the black and white balls and zipped them across the table into the pockets on the other end.

"*Au revoir, mes frères. Laissez le bon temps rouler.*"

She looked at me with that aggressive calmness of which she was uniquely capable. I followed her out of the room and then the front door of the house.

"I'm sorry, Vic. If you're finished with me and my smart mouth, I understand. I have said my peace . . . and then some . . . but I have no right to saddle you with it. I can make my way back to Louisiana on my own if you can drop me at a bus station."

Phil's introduction to my fraternity brothers had gone so well at first and then had turned into an uncomfortable disaster I could not have anticipated. If extreme confusion was a condition of being a *manboy*, the name fit me perfectly. I could not find any words for Phil as we walked to the car.

I did the only thing that felt right at that moment. I eased my foot off the brake that I continually pushed, and, without any words, took Phil's hand.

CHAPTER 8

A CONVOY of four National Guard troop trucks led by a jeep blocked the gate as Phil and I attempted to leave campus. An officer with a clipboard moved from truck to truck, first stepping up on the running boards to talk with the drivers and then going around to the back of the canvas-topped vehicles and barking out names.

"Sir," each guardsmen responded loudly when his name was called.

I left the car running but took it out of gear. I was in no hurry. I had no idea where I was headed. Wanting to let what had just happened at the fraternity house roll over in my mind, I looked for pertinent statements that had no hint of our mutually abhorred chit-chat.

"I've got a half t-t-tank of gas, but I didn't see many gas stations in Coldwater," I said. "I probably need to fill up b-b-before we leave Memphis."

Phil nodded.

The officer returned to the lead jeep and the trucks began to move out of the gate at a crawl. I would soon have to make a turn on North Parkway. Right? Left? If I went straight, I would end up in Overton Park. That's not so bad, I convinced myself.

"Are you thinking we should find a place to talk?" I asked Phil. "If that's what we need to do, the p-p-park is a quiet place." She turned to look at me.

"Good idea," she said, "but I need to throttle down my engines a bit. Let's go find some coffee first."

Maybe a little chit-chat wouldn't hurt after all. I needed a subject that Phil could take off on.

"How do you like the coffee up here in Memphis?" I asked. "I mean . . . compared to that g-g-good coffee in Louisiana."

"Seems to me it takes a lot of it to get you going. Next time I'll bring a bag of chicory with me," she said.

Next time. Were those words accidental? An unintended figure of speech? No matter. I took her "next time" as a gift.

THE OVERNIGHT CURFEW had ended at 6 a.m. The Toddle House we had visited on Thursday night had a half-dozen customers. Phil waited in the car as I went in to get two cups of coffee to go. The bacon and sausage sizzling on the table-sized griddle made me think guilty thoughts once again about leaving Nellie's cathead biscuits filled with juicy slices of country ham. I wrapped napkins around the hot paper cups and took them to the car where I handed Phil's to her through the window.

"How you gonna shift this doodle bug of yours with hot coffee in your hand?" she asked.

"I'll show you," I said proudly.

I reached under the driver's seat for my special cup holder. One of the publishing company's stereotypers, the group of printers who worked with the hot lead and built the half-round plates that went on the press, had made a unique cup holder for my car that consisted of a round lead base with four coat-hangar wires sticking straight up out of it around the edges. I positioned the contraption between my legs on the floorboard. The cup fit perfectly in the heavy lead base, preventing the coffee from tipping over. Phil was impressed.

"I need to get Daddy one of those for the boat," she said.

Phil sipped her coffee as I headed for Overton Park. The two cups of hot coffee fogged up the windows in the little car. I slid my window open.

"We have a lot of things that n-n-need talking about," I finally said, "but they may not be the same things."

"I'd say you're right about that, but you seem a little full up to me so why don't you go first when we get to some peace and quiet," Phil said. "And I'll see if I can't drop the sail on my too-smart mouth."

"Good plan . . . I m-m-mean about me going first," I said. "Not about your m-m-mouth."

Phil laughed. "You don't have to be so *précis*, Vic. We're not giving court depositions here."

Maybe not, but I had in my head that "court" was a good way to describe where I found myself with Phil.

THE NORTH ENTRANCE to the park near Southwestern had a double police barricade across it, so I drove to the main gate on East Parkway. Two Memphis cop cars blocked the entrance.

"We go to Southwestern," I told one of the officers, thinking for some reason that college status might give us privileges.

"Park's closed," one of the officers said. "You need to move on."

"B-b-but . . . ."

"Need to move on, son," the officer said, almost to my relief. I didn't have another point to argue. We weren't too far from my old house in midtown I had thought about taking Phil to see, but this wasn't a time for show-and-tell. We needed to talk face-to-face. Phil was waiting on me for a solution.

"Let's try that Tom Lee P-P-Park on the river that I showed you," I said. "Not many p-p-people go there, so there may not be any cops around to run us off and this little car will kind of be hidden."

Phil nodded. I turned right on to Poplar and headed west for the river, a geographical feature that we both appreciated and that I wanted to believe gave us something in common, although the river belonged to Phil more than it did me.

The traffic on weekend mornings on the main thoroughfares was normally on the light side, but few civilian vehicles could be spotted on this Saturday morning. Memphians apparently were staying in their homes, taking the city lockdown seriously.

Police, always with at least two officers in each car, roamed the streets at a crawl. National Guard trucks and jeeps were stationed at major intersections. We passed the fire station on South Main, the main hook-and-ladder company that served the tall downtown buildings. All the ladder trucks and pumpers were out front on the driveway. Firemen in over-sized rubber boots rolled up their heavy fire hoses. The firefighters obviously had been busy during the night.

Glass-repair trucks that usually hauled plate glass upright in racks were loaded instead with stacks of 4 X 8 plywood.

"Reminds me of the p-p-plywood that went up on houses in Louisiana when the hurricane was on the way," I said. The time I spent with Phil as Hurricane Betsy was on our tail had turned into one of the most thrilling events of my life. I thought about those days and nights often.

"All this plywood up here looks like light bread . . . brand new," Phil said. "We use plywood in Louisiana over and over until it turns gray. Daddy rebuilt most of our house with old plywood that we put up for the hurricane."

"I liked your house in V-V-Venice . . . a lot," I said. My comment sounded shallow, like so much small talk, but I trusted Phil knew that I meant it because I used the V-sound I hated so much.

"I'd like to see your house again . . . and V-Venice," I said. "Would like to do another *fais do-do* even, but I have to warn you that my d-d-dancing hasn't improved much. It's hard to believe it's been three years since I was d-d-down there . . . with you."

"Daddy's been trying to build the house back like it was, but somehow I don't think he has his heart in it," Phil said. "He finally got the charter business going again after Betsy, but I know he and Mama have been talking about selling out and moving the kids closer to New Orleans so everybody can find jobs. Mama says the kids are getting old enough that she can go back to work."

I could not imagine Phil without access to a charter boat and the Gulf of Mexico, her favorite place to escape the shackles of land.

"Do you still g-g-go out and help on your father's charters?"

"Not so much anymore with working my jobs and trying to get through my classes," she said, "but I might have a little more time . . . ." Phil stopped in mid-sentence and then continued. "At least for a few weeks."

"What's g-g-going to happen after a few weeks?" I asked. Phil waited a moment before she answered.

"I told them at the restaurant I wasn't going to be waitressing for them anymore 'cause more oil rigs are being built out in the Gulf and the helicopter fueling and servicing is picking up, with better money and a lot more interesting than waitressing and I'm close to being full-time with it."

It was not like Phil to run together her sentences, and she didn't attempt to answer my question.

"I'm glad you're staying in school," I said. "I guess you p-p-plan on going on to a four-year college."

I thought my comment would bring more conversation, but it seemed to end our discussion with a thud. Phil stared straight ahead in silence as we weaved through the downtown streets.

TOM LEE PARK, as I had hoped, was empty. My low-slung car would hardly be noticed from Riverside Drive. We took our coffees to an empty concrete bench that looked out over the river. A bench that Mr. Spiro and I had sat on countless times where he would explain the intricacies of the river and then, with his stories, carry me away to the ports of the world he had sailed to as a merchant marine.

At mid-morning a slight breeze was left from the night, but the Mid-South's humidity would be ramping up soon enough. Wednesday night's tornadoes that had brought the fresh air were long gone. Humid weather didn't wait until June to start in Memphis. The heat of summer started anytime it was good and ready.

"You're right about the river being **different** here," Phil said. "At home, it's hard for most outsiders to tell the river from the Gulf, but the Mississippi has high shoulders here, at least on this

Memphis side. The river here knows where it's going. The closer it gets to the gulf, the more *couillon* acting the river gets."

Phil scanned the Arkansas delta to the west and then north and south on the river.

"What are those new pilings up-river for?" she asked, pointing north.

"That's the new Hernando de Soto Bridge for Interstate 40 they s-s-started last year. It's going to s-s-stretch for three miles over into Arkansas, but most of that is over b-b-bottom land." I pointed downstream. "The old Memphis-Arkansas B-B-Bridge and the railroad bridge are each less than a mile long."

"I'm glad you know your way around the river up here," she said. "Most people don't think about the river." I was thankful anytime I could impress Phil.

River talk was there for the taking but I knew our dreaded heart-to-heart was nearing. I wanted to start it. To be the instigator. To be the first to take my foot off the brake. I considered easing into the conversation by saying "we have other fish to fry" but that euphemism soured in my mouth.

I took the only path I knew, diving straight in.

"From some of our c-c-conversations . . . from some of the things you said at the fraternity house . . . you think I'm a r-r-racist. Is that right?" Despite my clumsy effort, Phil was ready for me.

"It doesn't matter what I think, Vic. What do you think?"

When a conversation turned back on me, I became confused, much like the river as it made its way into the gulf.

"I think maybe . . . I could have been . . . some . . . but without r-r-realizing it," I answered in my best mealy-mouthed and non-committal way.

"Go on, then."

"But I never thought of Nellie as a s-s-servant . . . or a, you know, a maid. Only as a friend . . . a good friend I could talk to. My best friend, even."

"Go on, then."

"Everything m-m-might look one-sided because I never went to see her. . . and didn't write her all that much as the years went on. And you're right. I didn't know exactly how she m-m-made her living, and her age and things like that."

Phil didn't respond to my longer than usual sentences.

"But I still thought about her," I said. I waited for Phil to come back at me with something like "big deal," but she out-maneuvered me again with a simple question.

"So, do you think of her as your *égale* . . . your equal?"

"What do you m-m-mean?"

"Exactly what I asked. Do you think of her as your equal on this earth . . . as a human being?"

"Of course, she is," I said.

"Did you ever tell her?"

"Why should I have to t-t-tell her that?"

Phil did not hesitate.

"Because for her whole life everybody and every situation she has found herself in has been telling her different . . . that she doesn't have *égalité*. That she is a lesser being."

"How could anybody s-s-say that?"

"They don't have to say it. It's built in. *Automatique*."

Phil reloaded before I could get my mind around the depth of what she was saying.

 "You like your big words, so here's a good one for you *Institutionnelle*. Racial prejudice in this country runs deep, so deep that most people don't even realize it. And it's not going to change until people start thinking past themselves and correcting the old ways . . . the standard ways . . . of doing things."

My head was full. I watched the river and its current. I needed a break from the words. I got up to walk along the river, but I came back and stood in front of Phil, determined to keep up with her on her new tack that she had set for us.

"Maybe all it is . . . maybe it's just more s-s-selfish than racist," I said.

No hesitation again from Phil.

"Isn't that what racism is? Not being willing to share, to own up to what is rightfully due another person."

Phil was good at turning around a conversation with questions, so I gave it a try.

"So, do you think you, I mean, your family was d-d-discriminated against in Louisiana?"

Phil didn't answer as quickly this time. She took her time to construct her answer, which usually meant only bad news for me.

"Maybe not like Black people up here in Memphis, but we've had to put up with our share of *poodoo.* Like the slaves were taken out of Africa, our people were made to leave our homes in French Canada."

Phil's eyes told me she was building up a full head of steam.

"Maybe the only real difference between French-Cajuns and Blacks is that there wasn't as many of us for people to worry with. Nobody else in their right minds but us *coonasses* would move to the gator-infested swamps of Sout' Louisiana." Cutting off the "h" in "South" was the official Cajun pronunciation of her home.

"Think on this," she said. "When somebody sees me, I could be just another woman . . . a white woman with European blood from anywhere in the country. A Black person carries their *empreinte* with them wherever they go. Can't nobody hang a tag on me 'til I open my coonass mouth."

It was time to take a chance, not knowing if I was being insensitive or where my question would lead.

"Why did you c-c-call yourself a "coonass" at the fraternity house?"

"Probably shouldn't have, but sometimes my Cajun mouth runs ahead of my brain," she said. "But understand this . . . it's okay for a Cajun to call themselves a 'coonass', but can't anybody else use that word. *Comprenez vous?*"

I nodded, thankful I was never guilty of that. But Phil was not done.

"Other people try to paint a cute little face on 'coonass,' saying we got the name because our people once had to eat a lot of coons to stay alive in the swamps," she explained. "That ain't to be the truth, sure. It comes from the French word *connasse.* Take a guess at what that means."

I didn't have a clue. I shook my head.

"It means 'dirty whore.' "

Phil's in-my-face history lesson had begun to overwhelm me.

"Sorry to drop all that on you," Phil said. "I'm not a good date with all my smart-mouth preaching."

"Date" did not fit.

"I've never thought of you as a d-d-date," I said.

"Okay then, let's row that *pirogue*," she said. "Exactly how do you think of me?"

"Can we walk a little?" I asked.

We started to walk, and I knew I had to be careful with my answer. I was glad we were walking. Just like my speech improved when I was standing, walking seemed to help me line up my words if I could find some kind of rhythm with my words and feet.

"Well, you're a f-f-friend who's easy to talk to, fun to be around . . . someone who is not like any of my other friends . . . someone I would like to find a way to spend a lot more time with . . . someone I can learn from so I can be more expressive, if not in my words, at least in my . . . you know . . . writing."

I was proud of my answer, which was mostly non-stuttered. I decided to forge on.
"Someone who . . . "

Phil stopped and turned in her tracks, putting a gentle finger to my lips.

"Stop and think about what just came from your mouth. Think about your words and what they all have in common," she said.

I was stumped. I had no idea where Phil was going with this line of interrogation.

"I guess I was just s-s-saying that you make me more complete . . . that you add to me. That you do good things for me and make me b-b-better," I said. "I just feel b-b-better when I'm around you. Is that what you're talking about?"

"Exactly," Phil said. "It's all about what I can do for you, *mon cher*. Just like with Nellie Avant, who you say you care for so much. It's all about what she can do for you."

"Damn it, Phil. That's not fair . . . and you kn-kn-know it."

Phil grabbed me under my arm and started us walking along the river again.

"Don't start cursing at me again," Phil said, "cause you're lousy at it."

And then. "Might not sound fair to you, Vic, but it's *la vérité*."

The brake I was constantly pumping usually hid my hurt, but Phil was testing me harshly for a reason I could not understand. I had lashed out at her again, much like in the grocery store. I pulled away from her and quickened my pace. Phil did not try to catch up.

Did I finally understand Mr. Spiro's theory; the one which dictated that on the scale of emotions, the feelings of love and hate resided next to each other, not as opposite-points on the compass. If you loved somebody, did it mean it would be just as easy to dislike them as well? When confusion overwhelmed me as a boy, I retreated to the backyard where I would bounce a tennis ball off the garage doors for hours on end. I picked up small rocks from the path and flung them into the river. Rocks, unlike tennis balls, didn't offer the benefit of coming back to you.

Talking to Phil was exhausting, like running wind sprints after practice. Lost in my thoughts, I circled back to the car, Phil still following behind and letting me stew. *Drive. Just drive,* is all I could come up with as the silence hung over us.

As I slid into my car, I watched Phil as she stood before the monument to Tom Lee. Her hand reached out to touch the words near the bottom of the plaque—*Worthy Negro.*

WE PASSED the Greyhound Bus Station on Union Avenue. Phil pointed to it out her open window as she placed her left hand on top of mine.

"This is your last chance to put me on a bus back to Louisiana," Phil said. "I've got my bag back there in the trunk . . . and I'm ready to go if that's what you want."

So that was the reason she put her bag in the car at Nellie's house. Knowing that Phil didn't make idle threats, she was truly ready to get on the bus if that's what I wanted. Instead of answering, I pulled onto the first side street I came to, found a parking space and switched off the ignition.

"Okay . . . first, you're not going anywhere," I said with an unstuttered emphasis that was born of it being the only truth I knew at the moment.
"You just have to understand that I'm not good at answering your questions. I'm not using the right words. Not saying what I should be saying. I'm not used to talking with anybody about the things we talk about."

I could feel the worry-haints almost giggling, but at least I wasn't stuttering as much as usual. Then I felt unrehearsed and uncharted words come out of my mouth.

"I guess we're back to *only the ones who love you will tell you what you don't want to hear.*" I was more surprised at my words than Phil. "I'm sorry," I blurted out.

She smiled.

"*Mon Vic.* You are using the exact words you need to be using," she said. "You try to answer my intrusive and insulting questions with an absolute truth that is rare. By the time that most men are your age, they've learned how to hide their feelings. You have not acquired that talent . . . and let's hope you never do."

My head shook in the chaos of the conversation.

"You're confusing me," I said. "I f-f-feel like we're in some kind of a wrestling match of words, when all I want us to do is enjoy and get to know each other b-b-better while we have this chance."

"Let me help you out," Phil said, turning toward me in her bucket seat. She was back to that aggressive calmness that I had always admired and that I instinctively feared when I was in its path.

"If you had the good sense to ask me back there on the river exactly how I think about you, this is what I would say . . . you are a young man on your own for the first time and doing the best you can after having been given everything in a privileged life as an only child. You find it hard to give of yourself because you were raised only to know how to take. You let your stutter define you and that makes you unsure of yourself."

I did not look at Phil. I could tell she had a lot more for me, and for a reason I could not readily explain, this *manboy* was anxious to hear it. She continued.

"You're always looking to others . . . I'll go ahead and say it . . . you're looking to me to figure out who you should become instead of searching inside yourself. I do like to be around you because you are not satisfied with who you are, but understand me, Vic, you can't find the answers about who you are in others."

The parking lot was empty, and I felt corresponding emptiness inside me. I had nothing to say. Phil and I were still in a wrestling match of words, and she was putting the complete body slam on me.

"You have looked to others, like Mr. Spiro, for a sense of who you are. It's time you looked inside yourself."

I closed my eyes to keep the worry-haints from pouncing.

"I'm not going to say anything else, Vic, because I know I've hurt you, but listen to your own words — *only those who love you will tell you what you don't want to hear.*"

There was that word again. The one that was causing all the trouble. *Love.*

CHAPTER 9

I DON'T REMEMBER driving out of the empty parking lot. Phil's words continued to bounce around inside the convertible with the tape flapping in the wind like a flock of black birds. I felt like stopping in the middle of the street so that I could rip off all my pitiful attempts at patching the top and, likewise, rip out all the confusion inside me.

I soon found myself standing at the side of my car with a gas-pump nozzle in my hand. The gasoline running through the hose made the nozzle handle cool to the touch in the advancing heat of the warming Memphis day. The sensation of the cool pump handle brought me back to a measure of reality.

The service station, not too far from the newspaper plant, was one of the new types that let you pump your own gas instead of waiting on an attendant to come out and me having to say things like, "Fill it up with regular." I enjoyed the anonymity of the new self-serve stations. I nodded at the owner of the station who was cleaning his plate glass window. The friendly guy liked to joke with me about the size of the gas tank in my small car. I went inside to pay.

"I see you filled up that monster of a tank again," the station owner said with a chuckle. I nodded.

"Is that your lady out there?" he asked. Trying to make sense of questions myself, I had no answer for him.

"She's a right pretty one, ain't she?" I nodded.

"I bet you folks are busy up at the paper with all that's going on," he said. The station owner had always been kind and talkative. I felt bad doing so much nodding, selfishly not offering any words in return.

"Real b-b-busy," I said finally. "Have you had any trouble here at the station?" I didn't care to know, but I needed to make conversation with the talkative station owner.

"Cops came by yesterday and told me I could open up my pumps, but I couldn't sell no gas in a can to anybody," he said. "Only gas I can sell has to go directly into a car. One of my best customers came in this morning and tried to buy gas for his lawn mower and I had to tell him I couldn't sell it to him. He drove off spittin' mad. I might have lost a good customer from all this protesting mess."

"I guess they don't want people making b-b-bombs with gasoline," I said.

"I guess not. I'll be glad when all this riot business is over and things get back to normal," he said.

Normal?

Nothing in my life had been "normal" since Phil arrived at the train station Thursday afternoon. My intuition told me that any chance of normalcy would not return until she left on the train Monday morning. Even though our verbal wrestling was wearing on me, it was difficult for me to think about Phil leaving. Of her not being in my presence. Even though I had not seen her in three years, all my letters had kept me close to her because they afforded me the pleasure of thinking about her so much. Phil was right on one count. I used her for those three years. I didn't write those letters for Phil. I wrote them for me. Both the ones I sent and the ones I didn't.

"If you're still talking to me . . . where's the Lorraine Motel?" Phil asked as I slid into my seat with my thoughts continuing to run rough-shod inside me.

"Only a few b-b-blocks from here." I was thankful for any question that I could answer without going off an emotional high dive.

"I overheard a couple of men on the newspaper loading dock this morning saying that the reason that Dr. King was staying at the Lorraine Motel had something to do with a book," Phil said. "I guess I'm picking up your *habitude* of listening in on conversations." Phil was more apt to use her French when she wanted to express a negative, so I assumed the connotation of the word was "bad habit."

 "I wanted to talk to them more about that book, but your coffee was getting cold."

I wasn't much interested in the mysterious book, but the subject seemed worth pursuing, if only for the benefit of a conversation that might be non-confrontational.

"What's the b-b-book a-b-b-bout?" I asked.

When I was unsteady and my mind was racing, the consonants that gave me the most trouble were the B- and P-sounds. Speech pathologists called them "plosives" because the sounds required a buildup of air and then a release. My plosives did not line up correctly around Phil during our confrontations.

"I think they were saying it's a book that tells Black people where to stay overnight and where to eat in cities so they can avoid being *discriminée*."

"What's the name of the b-b-book?" I asked, in an attempt to sound engaged.

"It's a green book," Phil said.

I was confused but somewhat more intrigued.

"You mean the cover is green?" I asked.

"That's what I don't know," Phil said. "I wasn't all that clear about what they were telling me."

Decision time for me. Should I take Phil's lead and set out on a wild goose chase for a mysterious book that might or might not have a green cover? I decided it was better than being taken down in another of our verbal wrestling matches.

"Maybe . . . we should go to the Lorraine and ask around," I said. Phil perked up at my suggestion, even though I had no concept of what we were talking about or where this new direction might be heading.

"Let's give it a shoot," Phil said.

One of the endearing anacronyms of Phil's Cajun-French was the occasional disregard for past or present tense. A "shotgun" could just as easily be a "shootgun" in Phil's language that spontaneously ignored the rules of grammar. Her intellect knew full well the proper word was "shotgun," but her intuition mandated that once in a while that she should abdicate the norms that society tried to place on her.

Phil felt a freedom in her language that I didn't share in mine, and I was worrying that this constriction was carrying over into my writing. I told Phil in one of my many letters to her that I was having trouble with the third-person point-of-view. She wrote back a question that I will never forget: "Is not all writing first-person?" I started a letter back to her trying to explain the "POV" that my professor of rhetoric was always talking about. My explanations seemed ridiculous. I gave up. Maybe Phil was right, or as she would say, *c'est exact.*

I HAD PASSED the Lorraine Motel on Mulberry Street many times on my downtown runs for the newspaper.

The building itself was not distinctive, a typical two-story motel with plate glass windows that were covered on the inside by heavy beige drapes. What did stand out was the tall and colorful sign with the large red wing on top. As we approached the area, the display on the billboard portion of the sign called out. The plastic red letters said: "I have a dream. MLK." I wondered if those words were put there before or after the assassination.

I parked two blocks from the motel, as close as I could get. Yellow crime-scene tape cordoned off most of the motel's block on Mulberry. Marked and unmarked cars from city, state and federal agencies—even some city firetrucks—were parked haphazardly in the street, blocking Mulberry from through traffic even though it had been almost 48 hours since the fatal shot.

The *Press-Scimitar* had published a map on Friday that showed the location of the rooming house on South Main where the shot came from and where a suitcase and a rifle wrapped in a blanket had been found outside on the street. I pointed out to Phil the second-floor window of the flop house and then the second floor of the Lorraine where Dr. King collapsed in front of Room 306.

"The b-b-bullet traveled a distance of 205 feet, 3 inches, according to the map in the paper," I explained to Phil, remembering the exact numbers from the illustration done by one of the newsroom artists. I had rushed the pen-and-ink drawing done on heavy whiteboard down to the engraving department on the fourth floor myself on Friday morning, just after I had turned in my National Guard story.

"That's as long as our braided lines when we troll for tuna," Phil said. "Two-thirds the length of a football field. The assassin had to be either a professional or one lucky *connard*." My French vocabulary was lacking, but I could guess by the connotation that the word could be translated as "bastard."

Phil studied the area around the Lorraine.

"It does look kind of rundown around here, not like that big hotel not too far from the bus station," Phil said.

"That's the P-P-Peabody," I said. "Where those ducks swim in the fountain in the lobby."

"Wonder would he have gotten shot if he had been staying at that duck hotel?" Phil asked.

I shrugged, not giving the question an answer that it deserved.

Phil didn't seem to be intimidated as much as I was by the crime scene and the law enforcement presence surrounding it.

"Let's see if we can talk to somebody at the Lorraine about that book," she said.

"I doubt if we can get past the yellow p-p-police tape."

"You're a reporter," Phil shot back at me.

"I'm only a p-p-parttime copy clerk."

"They called you a 'staff writer' in that story you wrote about the National Guard at the college," Phil said. "That's a reporter in my book."

I knew the byline identification had been a mistake in the rush of deadline but arguing with Phil when she had her mind set was hopeless. I had played Phil's game of "find the book" for a good while now. I decided the only thing I could do was to see it through to its unlikely conclusion.

"Maybe I could show them my old p-p-press card that I used with the deputy in Coldwater," I said. I took it out of my billfold and stuck it inside a reporter's notebook. I felt between the seat and came up with a ball-point pen.

At that moment, I remembered Phil's bag in the trunk. If she was going to make me play this game, I decided that she might as well play too. I jumped out of the car, opened the trunk lid and took out Phil's shoulder bag and the newspaper's camera I had forgotten to return on Friday. Phil joined me at the rear of the car.

"Hang your b-b-bag on your shoulder and turn that logo to the inside," I said. "And strap this camera around your n-n-neck. You can play like . . . you know . . . you're a photographer . . . you know . . . my photographer." I relished calling her "my photographer" but not the way I had to sprinkle in a round of "you knows" just to get the words out.

If my spontaneous and off-the-wall instructions surprised Phil, she didn't show it.

"How do I look?" Phil said, adjusting the camera around her neck and the bag on her shoulder.

"Real . . . like a photographer," I said. A nice-looking photographer in a shape-affirming dress, I wanted to add but dared not.

"Are there any women photographers at the newspaper?" Phil asked.

"No, but there's a first time for everything," I said.

"You got that right, Sporty Boy."

I found relief in hearing those comfortable words again.

A NEWS STORY in Friday's *Press-Scimitar* had identified the owners of the Lorraine Motel as Walter and Loree Bailey. When the couple bought the hotel in 1945, Walter Bailey named the hotel in honor of his wife and the song "Sweet Lorraine," which Nat King Cole had recorded. Walter Bailey was quoted extensively in the story. If there was truly such a thing as a book of safe places for Black people to stay, it made sense that Mr. Bailey would know about it.

From my copy-clerk runs to the police station, I recognized some of the city patrolmen in blue uniforms. There were also some Shelby County sheriff deputies in khaki who manned the crime-scene area, but I didn't make runs to the state highway patrol offices on the outskirts of town much and didn't recognize any of the men.

One of the unexplainable tricks I used when I wanted to try to try to control my stuttering was to pretend to be someone else and to try to act and talk like that person might. What made a person sound like a real reporter from a newspaper? I was about to find out. I told Phil to walk a little bit to the side but behind me. Giving orders to Phil was new, especially telling her to walk behind me, but I had to make it look like I knew what I was doing and she seemed happy to oblige. After all, she was "my photographer."

"Good day," I said to the heavy-set state trooper. "I'm with the afternoon paper. I talked with the owner of the Lorraine, Mr. B-B-Bailey, about doing a feature story on his motel and he said I could come by the m-m-motel and talk to him."

The trooper looked me over and then stared at Phil.

"This is my photographer," I said, casually motioning over my shoulder, in what I hoped was my best newspaper-reporter voice.

"Need to see some ID," the trooper said.

I opened the notebook, handed him my press card and pulled my driver's license from my billfold.

"How 'bout you," he said to Phil. She didn't miss a beat.

"Just started at the newspaper," Phil said. "First job out of school." Her smile and demeanor took me back to how she interacted with the older men who chartered her father's boat and how she could turn on her *fais do-do* dazzle at a moment's notice.

"You got any ID?" he asked.

"Just my driving license, sure," Phil said, ramping up her French-Cajun accent. She reached inside her phony camera bag.

"Where you from, Miss?" the trooper asked.

"Louisiana. Plaquemines Parish. Went to school in La-fa-yette." She pronounced the city in three emphatic syllables as only a French-Cajun was capable of.

"We don't see many lady photographers up this way," the trooper said to Phil, not trying to hide his enjoyment in talking with her.

"You see me," Phil said. "One of me is all you need, sure."

I'm not certain what Phil meant, but it didn't matter. The trooper smiled. Phil had set the hook and was reeling him in.

"Let me go talk to my captain. Wait here behind the tape." The trooper ambled off toward the motel office.

The two-way radios from the cars and walkie-talkies around the crime scene cackled with static and truncated transmissions. Phil and I watched the trooper talk to his boss and then he handed him our IDs. The trooper started back towards us.

"We may be dead meat," I whispered to Phil.

"Keep it going, Sporty Boy," she said softly. "We can do it."

The trooper came to the yellow tape and raised it for us to slide under.

"Go to the office door there and check in with the captain," he said. "He's got your IDs."

"Welcome to Tennessee, Miss Moreau," the trooper said, as she ducked under the yellow tape. "Did I say your name correctly?"

Phil smiled and nodded to the officer. "Thanking you, Mr. Nice Highway Patrolingman." Phil touched the camera hanging around her neck. "You catch somebody and I'll be taking your picture good, sure."

I winced when Phil said "picture" instead of "photo." Newspaper photographers "shot photos," they didn't "take pictures." With Phil talking in her exotic dialect, however, the words didn't seem to matter.

If conversing with the state trooper had tested all my skills of stealthy entry into a crime scene, the captain was a new challenge. Phil's South Louisiana charm and my press card didn't seem to have much impact at this higher rank.

The captain was all questions and roadblocks. What kind of story was I working on? Why didn't I just wait for the afternoon press briefing and ask my questions then? All press inquiries had to be funneled through the FBI who had taken over the investigation. When exactly had I talked to the motel owner? He finally shared with us that Mr. Bailey was not on the premises.

I was losing momentum with each question I tried to answer and every argument I could think to present. I was ready to collect our IDs and go when Phil jumped in.

"*Capitaine*, sir, this is just a little story to tell some of the history of this Lorraine Motel. Not many locals know about this place, and it might be good to do something *positif* to help quiet things down," Phil said. She pointed through the glass door. "I see the desk clerk there. We can just talk to him, and I'll take a picture of the lobby and we'll be out of your way quick like, sure."

"Absolutely no photos allowed inside the tape," the captain said sternly. "This is a federal crime scene."

"Could I just speak with the desk clerk there and see when Mr. B-B-Bailey might be available again by phone?" I asked, trying to pry open the small crack that Phil had opened for me. "My photographer can just wait here . . . with you . . . if you don't allow photos."

The captain looked at the clerk, a middle-aged Black man, sitting on a stool behind the reception desk with his chin resting in one hand, a newspaper spread out before him.

"Five minutes. That's it," the captain said. "You're not to go anywhere else. Stay where I can see you. If you're not back out here in five, I'll come and drag you out. I'll wait out here with your photographer to make sure she doesn't take any photos."

Phil played her new role as a newspaper photographer flawlessly. She took the camera from around her neck and sat down on a sidewalk curb near the door.

The clerk slid off his stool as the captain opened the door for me. Mr. Bailey was at the hospital with his wife, the clerk informed me. She had collapsed shortly after she heard that Dr. King had been shot and still was in serious condition. I scribbled that new information in my notebook and would give it to the city desk.

"I'm with the afternoon paper. Do you know anything about a b-b-book that has lists of where Black people can safely get a room?" I asked the clerk. "I think it may have a green cover."

He reached under the desk. "You mean this?"

I looked at the well-worn paperback book with the green cover. *The Negro Travelers' Green Book – 1959 Edition. Guide for Travel & Vacations.* Across the bottom of the cover: *Carry your Green Book with you . . . you may need it.*

"Could you let me borrow this so I could make some copies at the p-p-paper? I'll get it right back to you."

The clerk was already shaking his head before I finished.

"No sirree," the clerk said. "Mr. Bailey says that book stays right here and I'm not to let it out of my sight."

Arguing with a stranger was hopeless for me. I could only stare at the clerk. He continued his side of the argument.

"Mr. Bailey say these books is hard to come by."

I managed to ask the clerk if I could quickly flip through it. He reluctantly handed it to me. The small book was 90 pages and printed on cheap paper. I made mental notes as I flipped through the books. On page 2 was a paragraph about how Blacks could send in for a "travel identification card" and there was a section on how to protect your home while you were away. The states were alphabetical. The Lorraine Motel at 406 Mulberry Street was listed on page 63.

On the title page, a Victor Hugo Green was credited as the book's founder.

"Do you kn-kn-know if it's called the "Green Book" because it has a green cover or b-b-because the man who first started it is named "Green?" I asked the clerk.

"Don't know 'bout that," the clerk said. "Mr. Bailey said that Green man had passed on anyway. Mr. Bailey says the man's wife is the one who puts it out now."

Alma D. Green was listed as the editor and publisher. I got out my notebook and jotted down the address and telephone number in New York City.

"I'd say this book brings lots of folks in here," I said to the clerk. "Anybody I would know . . . b-b-besides Dr. King?"

"I'd say so," the clerk said. "How 'bout Ray Charles, Louis Armstrong, Nat King Cole, young girl singer named Aretha Franklin." I scribbled down the names.

"You know 'bout Isaac Hayes?" the clerk asked.

I nodded. The newspaper had just carried a feature story on the musician.

"He comes by all the time to sit by the pool and eat Mrs. Bailey's fried chicken," the clerk said. "He said there weren't any better."

The captain rapped on the glass door. I had seen Phil keeping him in steady conversation.

"Thank you much," I said to the clerk. "Tell Mr. B-B-Bailey 'hello' for me and that I hope his wife gets better." I had to remind myself that I had never talked to Mr. Bailey.

The captain opened the door and motioned, letting me know my time was up.

"Thanks for your help, Captain," I said. "I'll be talking to Mr. B-B-Bailey . . . again . . . later on."

He handed our IDs back to us.

"Remember the press briefing at 4 p.m. Usual place," he said.

"Anything new?" I asked, finding myself more comfortable in the persona of a reporter.

"Not that I know of," he said, "but the FBI don't tell us locals much . . . don't quote me on that. That's off the record."

I smiled and nodded.

Back at the car, Phil stowed the camera and her shoulder bag in the trunk.

"Well, that was more fun than a *rodeo*," Phil said, making the word sound unusually exotic. "Did you get much out of that clerk?"

"Not a lot," I said, "but I saw a copy of the *Green Book*. It actually has a green cover and it's real. He wouldn't let me b-b-borrow it . . . but I found out something that's interesting. I think it's called the *Green Book* because the author's name is Green. Victor Hugo Green."

"Where have I heard that name . . . Victor Hugo?" Phil asked.

"He was the French guy who wrote *Les Miserables*," I said. "Mr. Spiro talked a lot about his writing."

"*Les Miserables*," Phil said, but in a pronunciation that made mine sound inappropriate. "I remember now. I haven't read it, but I think I probably should."

I didn't want to sound too excited, but I needed to give Phil credit for encouraging me to step out of my comfort zone.

"I almost, in fact, I did enjoy that," I said. "You know . . . b-b-being a reporter for a change."

"'Reporter in French is *journaliste*," Phil said. "The way you're always writing, I'd say you got the journaling part down. You just need to ease up and not be so afraid to talk to people more."

"You mean . . . like take my foot off the b-b-brake," I said.

Phil smiled. "I guess maybe you could say it like that."

Phil took the camera from around her neck and put it in the trunk with her bag.

 "What was that clerk's name?"

"Oh . . . I forgot to ask," I said sheepishly.

"You're some reporter, sure," Phil said, accompanied by one of her taunting laughs. "I'm wishing now I had gotten in there to take some pictures."

"You're some photographer, sure," I said, attempting my best Cajun rejoinder. "Only thing . . . there's no film in the camera."

She playfully tapped me with her overnight bag. We both laughed. Sharing a laugh with Philomene Moreau was a healing.

EVEN WITH THE MANHUNT for the assassin going on, the *Press-Scimitar* newsroom was empty on Saturday afternoon since the paper didn't publish a Sunday edition.

I typed a note to the city desk saying that Loree Bailey, an owner of the Lorraine Motel along with her husband, was in the hospital after collapsing when she heard that Dr. King had been shot. I had not seen that reported anywhere.

Phil found the Saturday edition of *The Commercial Appeal.* The bold headline in all caps across the top of the page read:

RIOTERS RAVAGE MAJOR CITIES

A large wire photo showed flags in Washington at half-staff.

"Do you mind if I type another quick note?" I asked Phil. "It won't take long."

"I'm in no hurry," Phil said. "Except we do need to find us some lunch. I don't want to go back to Nellie's and eat up all her food."

"I've got the perfect place," I said. "You'll love it. Just hang on."

My note was a two-parter to Chis. I asked him if he thought the city desk would be interested in a story from me about the reason that Dr. King was staying at the Lorraine Motel. The second part of the note was more personal. I wanted to know if he thought there was any chance that I could get a fulltime—and paid—internship as a reporter starting in June when my semester ended. I underlined "paid" with a black editing pencil. I sealed the note in an envelope and put it in Chis's mail slot.

"Ready," I said to Phil. "I'm taking you to the best barbecue place in Memphis."

She folded the newspaper she was reading.
"You need to be watching your money since you're in the poorhouse like the rest of us church mice," Phil said. "We can just get some coffee and share a plate of fries somewhere."

"Not today," I said. "I've got some overtime pay coming and you're gonna love this barbecue. It's almost as good as your mother's jambalaya."

Phil shot her critical laugh at me.

"Let's not get too *sûr de toi*. Nothing *compare* to my mama's

jambalaya."

Phil was back to her habit of gigging me generously with her French phrases. I treasured each one.

Chapter 10

LEONARD'S PIT BARBECUE on South Bellevue was on the way back to Coldwater. The restaurant was my father's favorite. We often stopped there on our trips to the family cabin on Moon Lake and bought enough pulled-pork barbecue and ribs to last the weekend.

When the waitress asked if Phil wanted the slaw "on or off," I jumped in to explain that a Memphis pork barbecue sandwich needed to be eaten with the slaw "on" the bun, not on the side.

"When in Rome," Phil said, adding emphasis to the guttural "R," one of those complex linguistic manipulations that had led to my downfall in French class.

I ordered my father's favorite, the half n' half plate—half barbecue and half spaghetti.

"That's like mixing shrimp and crawfish," Phil said. I explained how much my father liked the combination.

"You never mentioned your parents in your letters, and you don't talk about them much," Phil said. "Do you still see them?"

"My father calls some but, he's b-b-busy in New Orleans trying to get his new b-b-business going," I said.

"How 'bout your *maman?*"

Phil's French-Cajun word for "mother" sounded endearing and full of familial affection.

"I see her some, but we don't get . . . don't talk much," I said.

Our so-called "family unit" of three was not like Phil's with two inseparable parents who had grown stronger together as they raised their five children in the swamps of hardship in South Louisiana. I had only been with the Moreau family for a few days, but the bond and respect they shared for each other was apparent in everything they did.

The thought came to me that this was the first time I had eaten at Leonard's that my father was not with me. I pushed away my half-eaten plate.

"Is there a *problème?*"

"Probably . . . yes. But I can't . . . ." I tried to shake the conversation out of my head that I was having with myself. I needed to find the words to put my roller-coaster thoughts to rest.

"In my p-p-part of the South if you want to make believe that something didn't happen, you just don't talk about it."

Phil wasn't about to let me off that easy with an answer that was accurate but that contained no information.

"So, what I hear you say is that you aren't going to talk about whatever is pestering you. *Comprenez-vous?*"

I nodded.

I did want to talk about the fact that I didn't know who my biological father was, but I didn't know how.

Phil let me off the hook with questions about the newspaper. I was surprised that I could answer most of them with some confidence. I began to explain some of the finer points of newsroom politics, including the growing controversy between management and staff created by race identification in crime reports.

"You're a good *journaliste*, like a sailor," Phil said. "Always watching the wind and compass."

I was not a reporter . . . yet . . . officially, but Phil's simile gave me a sense what might be possible.

We didn't talk much on the drive back to Nellie's, but the silence did not come from the worry-haints picking at me. Conversations in my car at highway speeds were difficult with all the noise from the disheveled top. It was the middle of the afternoon and we had been up since 3 a.m. Phil leaned back in her seat and closed her eyes.

Spending time with my thoughts and no conversation was a gift. Around the edges of all that had gone on—at the fraternity house, at the Lorraine Motel, at Tom Lee Park—I could feel a new course taking shape. A new compass heading, Phil might say.

I didn't have all the pieces to the plan worked out yet, but my new resolve was that I would not let go of Phil easily. My reason for inviting her to Memphis, besides her accurate and hurtful observation that I wanted to show her off at the fraternity, was simply to have the chance to see her again, but I felt now that there was more at stake, even with all our issues that her visit was bringing into the open. In a strange way, the rough patches we were experiencing made me feel even closer to her. That short distance between love and hate.

As Phil napped with her head to one side, I grew more excited about new possibilities, along with the realization that the worry-haints were not pestering me as much. I could feel my foot easing off the brake and putting it on the gas pedal of my thinking. Rat would have been proud.

TO MY SURPRISE, we saw a blonde-haired girl sitting at Nellie's feet on the front porch when we drove into the yard.

"Oh, good. Blythe is here after all," Phil said, looking through my dirty windshield.

Nellie was working on one of her needle stories with Blythe watching intently. Nellie put away her cloth and thread and walked Blythe down the porch steps to greet us.

"Glad you two is back," Nellie said. "Miss Phil has met Blythe, but I don't think you have, Vic."

"Nice to meet you, B-B-Blythe," I said, smiling and nodding but keenly aware that the plosive "B" was one of my greatest hurdles. She stared at me.

"My name is Blythe . . . not B-B-Blythe." I tried to hide my embarrassment from Phil. Nellie quickly jumped in.

"Ain't Miss Blythe a right pretty one?" Nellie said.

I smiled and nodded.

"We have six chickens," Blythe said to me, holding up three fingers on one hand and three on the other. She stared at me. "Do you like chickens?"

"I like them, but I don't care too much for that rooster," I said, relieved that I had come up with a spontaneous joke but more relieved that I had hidden my stutter from Blythe.

"Roosters are just boy chickens. Why don't you like them?" Blythe asked with a sad look.

"No, I like chickens fine . . . and roosters too," I said.

"Chickens lay eggs, but roosters can't," Blythe said.

Nellie rescued me once again.

"Miss Blythe can tell you anything you wants to know about chickens," Nellie said. "And most other animals. She likes to go to the zoo as much as you did when you was a little man."

I glanced at Phil who was smiling.

"You should hear Blythe talk to her chickens," Phil said. "She has named them and they cock their heads when she calls their names."

"Minnie. Mary. Martha. Margaret. Maggie. Missy," Blythe said. "Because chickens are girls."

Phil took Blythe's hand.

"Let's go 'round back to see the girls," Phil said.

Blythe smiled. They walked around the side of the house, swinging hands.

"I don't think I'm g-g-going to do all that well talking to B-B-Blythe," I said to Nellie.

"You'll learn to know her ways when you stay around her long enough," Nellie said. "That sweet girl thinks her own thoughts in her own special ways. I love her to the heavens."

Nellie explained that the family car had brought Blythe over unexpectedly during the morning because her father and mother had to go to Memphis to see about the family businesses there. They would be staying at their house in Memphis and didn't want to take Blythe into the city with all the violence that might upset her. They wouldn't be back until Sunday afternoon, so Blythe would be spending the night at Nellie's.

Nellie informed me that she had already worked out the sleeping arrangements. Blythe in Nellie's room on the pallet. Phil would have the sofa in the front room and Nellie had asked Bernice to bring over some more quilts so I could make a soft pallet next to Phil.

Could not have made a better plan myself, I thought. For completely selfish reasons, I was excited that Blythe would be spending the night in Nellie's room so Phil could spend the night in mine.

Phil came around the side of the house.

"Blythe wants to go pick some Forget-Me-Nots on the levee," Phil said. "We won't be gone long."

"Take your time," Nellie said. "Me and Vic rightly need to do some catching up."

Exactly what I had been thinking.

THE NEEDLE STORY that Nellie had been working on when I arrived was spread out on the back of her straight-back chair on the porch. She was just getting started on a new one. Nellie would do her needlework on any piece of white cloth she could find, mostly now on pieces of old bed sheets. I recalled her saying when she lived with us that old flour sacks were the best because the rough weave made for easier sewing, but flour had stopped coming in cloth sacks. Nellie's recent creations had taken on a more impressionistic look.

"What's this story going to be about?" I asked, handing the cloth gently to Nellie.

She held it up and looked at it from different angles.

"I had a mind it might be the pharaoh's chariots and soldiers being swallowed up when the Red Sea closed up on them, but my horses tend to look to look a mite like dogs or cows," Nellie laughed. "I guess that won't matter none to Miss Blythe."

"My favorite needle story of yours is the one you did about M-M-Moses and the burning bush," I said. "I thought about that story when I read that Dr. King said in his speech that he had seen the P-P-Promised Land."

"I have no doubt that he saw that glory land. Saw it plain as day," Nellie said.

"Do you think he had the feeling that he would d-d-die so soon . . . the very next day?"

Nellie studied her thread and cloth on the front and back while preparing her answer.

"I believe he was a right saint who knew the power of God and maybe he could feel things sharper than most of us because of that," Nellie said. "He knew his days were coming to a close like everybody's does and he wanted to make sure that we would be okay to continue on without him being on this earth."

We had learned in rhetoric class about the importance of closing statements and completion. For every conversation, Nellie seemed to have a proper ending.

"He's not gone in my mind," she said. "He's just gone on ahead."

I gave her words silence and the proper space they deserved.

"Can you still thread your needle and sew with either hand?"

Nellie smiled from her chair and nodded.

"I remember that my m-m-mother used to tell her friends that you were *amphibious*, when she meant *ambidextrous*," I said. Nellie smiled again.

"They knew that she meant I was either-handed," Nellie said, folding up her needle story in the basket that contained a mishmash of brightly colored thread.

One of the rudiments of conversation I was trying to learn was how to ease into subjects carefully. Mr. Spiro had told me that I had not learned how to beat around the "proverbial bush."

"Nellie, can I ask you if you thought my p-p-parents treated you fairly when you were living with us . . . and did I treat you . . . you know . . . like I should have?"

"What might you be speaking to exactly?" Nellie asked, continuing to separate the different colors of thread on the edge of her sewing basket.

"That room you lived in over the garage wasn't all that nice . . . and my p-p-parents didn't pay you much like they should have."

"Understand me now," Nellie said. Her admonition of "understand me" was Nellie's gentle way of scolding and her desire to set the record straight.

"I had everything I needed. Mr. V was all the time slipping me dollars that no one knew about, including your mama. I never wanted for anything, then or since."

"B-B-But . . . you had to go back to Coldwater with n-n-nothing when we moved into our new house," I protested.

"Yo' mama paid my bus ticket and Mr. V gave me a goodly sum of money to get by on for a time," Nellie said.

"You should have gotten more," I said.

Nellie shook her head. "Now, don't you go making up my shoulds for me."

This line of conversation was going nowhere. I needed to change course.

I peppered her with questions about her time living with us in Memphis until she finally had enough of me quizzing her.

"You're full of too many questions about the past, Vic," she said. "The prophet Isaiah says not to dwell on what's gone by. Only today is important. If you don't live for today, all you have is a bunch of yesterdays."

"I feel bad that I didn't think about your s-s-situation more . . . that I was too busy playing b-b-ball and thinking about myself and the big p-p-problems I thought I had," I said. "Phil asked me how old you were, and I couldn't even tell her."

With my confession, Nellie put down her sewing basket and went inside. She returned with her Bible that I recognized from

Memphis. The once-black leather cover had worn down to more of a mottled gray. She opened it to a bookmark made from the thin wooden handle of one of the fans she would bring home from her church in Memphis. At the top of each page of her Bible were consecutive numbers written carefully by hand. She pointed to the last number—28,502.

"This is the present number of how many days I have been on this earth," Nellie said. "Every morning that the Lord allows me to wake, I put down in my Bible the next number in line. This is the number I wrote down this morning. I don't pay much mind to months and years. I only take it by the day."

I asked to see her Bible and thumbed through the pages. Around the margins on each page were sequential numbers written in pencil in her crude but consistent hand. I vaguely recalled seeing the numbers on the pages in Memphis, but I had never asked about them.

"Some say a body is not supposed to write in the Bible, but my mama wrote in hers every day," Nellie said.

 I couldn't do the calculation in my head, so I pulled my notebook and pen from my back pocket. I divided 28,502 by 365.

"That makes you more than 78 years old," I said.

"Thereabouts, I reckon," Nellie said. "I don't keep up with it like that. My mama started me out by counting the days for me and writing them in the Bible, and that's what I kept up with through my years. Folks might try but can't nobody live more than one day at a time."

I began doing quick calculations in my head. Nellie was around 63 when she came to live with us in Memphis. She was 65 years old when she yanked me out of the storm drain in front of our house when Rat or none of my neighbors could get me out. She was nearing 70 when she returned to Coldwater and picked orphan cotton in the fields behind the mechanized cotton-pickers.

"You haven't had much of a life," I said. "And I'm s-s-sorry I'm just now coming around to realize that."

"Now, listen to me strictly," Nellie said, taking back her Bible. "My God has given me a full life. I want for nothing. God provides for everything I need . . . and we're not going to have any more of this kind of talk about what has passed, about what is done."

A living wage. Social Security. Proper medical care. God didn't provide these, I wanted to protest, but then Nellie silenced me.

"My family might have come from the plantations, but I am a slave to no one on this earth. I have lived a blessed life and will not be made into something I am not."

I sat on the edge of Nellie's porch, lost in the thoughts of my selfish 21 years and the realization that Phil could have been much harder on me if she had known all of Nellie's story.

LOST IN MY THOUGHTS while sitting on the edge of the porch, I brushed at something on my head. Blythe stood behind me, pinching the petals off the Forget-Me-Nots and dropping them on me one at a time. I turned to see Phil at the screen door. Smiling.

"My chickens don't like to eat flowers, so I'm putting them on your head," Blythe said. "Is that okay?"

"Okay, you bet," I said. "At least my head is good for something." Blythe smiled at my obscure joke.

Blythe held a bouquet of shredded flowers in her hand. She picked off the small petals and blew them from her fingers.

"If you blow the flowers into the air, they will land on the ground and come back again pretty next year," Blythe said. "It says so in Miss Nellie's Bible."

Nellie followed Phil through the screen door.

"I told Miss Philomene I would cook us up some dinner, but she said you was planning to go out to eat somewhere since your college party in Memphis was called off," Nellie said.

I nodded, trying to come out of my daze and catch up with whatever plans that Phil had made without me.

"Didn't you tell me there were some places to eat over at that Moon Lake?" Phil said. "How far is that from here?"

"Maybe 45 minutes," I said.

"Moon Lake. That's where I fly on the water," Blythe chattered.

"That's right. Miss Blythe and her family has a place and a boat on Moon Lake like your parents have," Nellie said.

"Had," I said. "My father sold it after the d-d-divorce."

The levee hid the sunset. I checked my watch.

"I think I do remember a place to eat at Moon Lake, if it's still there," I said.

"Fly over the water," Blythe said. "I can fly over the water."

"Oh, you m-m-mean like water skiing," I said to Blythe.

She nodded. "Yes. Flying over the water."

"I liked to ski too . . . fly over the water . . . at Moon Lake," I said. I was learning the knack of talking to Blythe like Nellie had assured me I would.

MOON LAKE was created when the Mississippi River changed directions thousands of years ago, probably due to an earthquake. The ox-bow lake was left stranded in the Mississippi Delta. The *Press-Scimitar* had a thick file on the popular lake that I liked to thumb through in my spare time. I had enjoyed summers at our cabin there with my friends and family, when there had been a family.

The eastern shore of the lake had once been a popular place for summer homes for Memphians. My father liked to fish although he only had time to go once or twice each summer. I spent all my time water-skiing on the lake with friends. I was pleased that I had translated Blythe's "flying over the water."

The only restaurant I remembered from my family's time on the lake was called Conway's, named after some country-western singer born in Mississippi who bought the place for his parents to operate in retirement. My parents had talked about meeting friends at Conway's and said the food was not bad. I had never been inside.

Phil seemed to be in a good mood for a change. She asked me to put the top down on my car to keep the flappy tape from making so much noise. Dusk had a way of chasing away the humidity in the country with no concrete to hold in the heat. Even though we were less than an hour from Memphis, the quiet backroads of Mississippi seemed far removed from what was going on in the city. Phil said she enjoyed her walk with Blythe on the levee, and that talking with Blythe was exciting, never knowing what she would say and wondering where her thoughts came from.

"Her conversation seems to be a kind of s-s-stream of consciousness," I said. "It's like she has no brakes on anything that might come in her mind."

"I guess that's how you writers would describe it," Phil said.

I couldn't decide if "you writers" was pejorative or approbative when Phil used it, and I wasn't about to ask. I enjoyed being labeled a writer, even though all I had to show for it was some ripped up short stories, dozens of letters—sent and unsent to Phil—and one story published in the newspaper.

MOST OF THE RESTAURANTS from years ago along the shore of Moon Lake had closed. Some of the places had been called "supper clubs," which, my father had explained, meant that members could buy liquor there and there was usually a band of some kind. I had been to a glorious *fais do-do* underneath the Moreau house in Louisiana. If there was entertainment at Conway's—if the restaurant was even still operating—I doubted it could match that special night in Venice, Louisiana, that played over and over in my mind like a scene from a favorite movie.

To my relief, a few cars and pickup trucks were parked haphazardly in the gravel parking lot of Conway's. The building reached out over the water on spindly posts. The damp smell of the shallow-water lake was familiar and the cypress knees resembled ancient sculptures.

"Need to see some ID from you kids," the middle-aged waitress said as she led us to a table. I handed her mine, proud I was finally of legal age in Mississippi to order a beer.

Phil still had on her dress with no pockets. She told the waitress her driver's license was in her bag in the trunk of the car. The waitress looked her over. "You'll pass for 21, sweetie, even if you're not," the waitress said.

"*Merci beaucoup*," Phil replied.

"Well, thanks, darling. I guess," the waitress said with a quizzical look. She handed us menus and said she would be back to take our order.

About half the Linoleum-topped tables in the dining room were occupied, mainly with older couples. Several men congregated on stools at a long bar. We ordered fish platters.

"What's on tap?" Phil asked the waitress.

"We got several kinds, dearie," the waitress said.

"How 'bout Dixie?"

"Don't reckon we got that one, honey."

"Doesn't matter then," Phil said. "Pull me what you got."

"I'm sorry your big *soirée* got called off," Phil said after the waitress left.

"I guess I'm not," I said. "Doesn't seem exactly right that an Old South B-B-Ball should be going on the weekend after Dr. King was killed. Does it?"

"You answer your own question," Phil said. "You're the one who asked it."

I should have let it go at that or beat around the bush, but I was still learning the ins and outs of conversation with Phil and more anxious to ease my foot off the brake.

"Phil, you said all I wanted to do was show you off to my fraternity b-b-brothers . . . and there's some truth to that . . . and I'm sorry," I said. "But I realized when I saw you get off the train that all I wanted was to, you know, be with you and talk to you."

Phil laughed.

"All right now, Sporty Boy, let's don't start offering confessions here on a Saturday night," she said. "You know I'm a good Catholic girl and we save those for Sunday morning mass. Let's just have us a good time tonight."

Phil was right. Wrong place. Wrong time. Wrong kind of conversation.

Three older Black men walked through a door beside the bar and took their places among the instruments on a makeshift bandstand in a far corner of the dining room. The name on the bass drum was "The Nighthawks." The piano player who sat behind an electric keyboard that seemed held together with packaging tape introduced the band as the "Jelly Roll Kings." The third man played a bright red electric guitar plugged into a small amplifier.

We listened to the first few songs as we ate. Phil said she liked the music more than she thought she would.

"I thought you said this was a country-western place," Phil said. "This sounds more like Bourbon Street blues to me." Her French pronunciation of "bourbon" made it sound other-worldly.

I commenced telling Phil about a conversation with Rat from years ago when I had told him that music around Memphis was "eclectic."

"You mean 'electric,'" he had said. I explained to him what the word "eclectic" meant. From that day on, Rat told anyone who would listen and with a big smile that he was going to learn to play the "eclectic guitar." I wished that Rat, wherever he was now, could meet Phil. They would like each other. Neither one had any brakes.

Phil had eaten only about half her fried fish when she pushed her plate back and took a long drink of beer from her glass.

"Don't fill up too much on food so you won't be able to dance," she said. "I've got an *envie* to, how you say, cut us some *tapis*."

Instead of protesting that my dance skills were lacking, I knew what I had to say. "Fair warning. You know what you're g-g-getting into . . . so it's all your fault."

"I'll take all the blame," she said as she grabbed my hand and pulled me to the floor in front of the band.

Dancing with Phil reminded me of when my father would switch his airplane over to autopilot. I didn't have to think about what I was doing when I danced with Phil. I simply followed her and everything seemed to work out the way it should. When Phil twirled, she made it look like I was twirling her. She literally danced circles around me. To my mind I wasn't actually dancing but it probably seemed like it to anybody watching us. The other patrons in the restaurant ignored us. None joined us on the floor, an oddity that seemed fine with Phil. After a few fast numbers, Phil walked over to chat with the keyboard player. I went back to our table for a sip of beer. She motioned me back to the dance floor.

"They promised me a slow dance," she said.

The only other time I had danced with Phil was underneath her house in Venice that was built high above the ground on posts. The dance floor had been an assembly of some plywood sheets that would eventually be used to board up the house ahead of the hurricane. We were alone after the *fais do-do*. It was a night lived over and over when I missed Phil and gave myself over to thinking about her. At last, after three long years, I held Phil again and somehow, without much help from me, we moved as one as the Jelly Roll Kings played their eclectic music on their electric instruments.

The worry-haints were never far away, however, even as I held Phil close. I had only met Phil a few hours earlier the first time I saw her dance. All the men wanted to dance with her and be around her. I found myself growing jealous and I barely knew the Louisiana girl . . . the Louisiana woman. I resented anyone touching her. Although we never discussed the subject, I assumed she had dated other men in the three years we had not seen each other. The worry-haints had gotten to me so bad at one point that in one of my letters I asked her to tell me about the men she was dating, but I tore up the letter in a fury and flushed the pieces down the toilet at the fraternity house, trying to drown the worry-haints. True to my southern upbringing, if I wanted to pretend that something didn't happen, I knew not to talk about it.

THE MEN crowded at the bar at Conway's laughed and talked increasingly louder while the band was on break. Most of the couples had finished their meals and some had resituated with their drinks to the club's screened-in porch that jutted out over Moon Lake.

Phil and I decided that since we had gotten up at 3 a.m. we wouldn't wait for the band to return, even though Phil said that she had truly enjoyed their music. She excused herself to go to the ladies room through the doors at the end of the bar.

As she passed the group of men, all dressed in jeans with substantial bellies protruding over their belts, she stopped suddenly at the loud laughter, shaking her head. She turned around to look at me and then went through the door to the restrooms. I didn't try to hear what the men were talking about, still reveling in the sensation of holding Phil close to me on the dance floor.

I paid the tab and left a good tip on the table, not so much for the service or the food but instead for the restaurant that gave me the privilege of dancing with Phil. The men at the bar continued to drink and laugh. Phil came back to our table with that look of intense calm on her face; that same look I had seen several times on the river as the current raged and the pre-hurricane winds blew.

"Listen to me close. I want you to go and stand near the door where we came in," Phil said.

"Why?" I asked. "What are you going to do?" I could sense that I was not going to get a complete answer.

"I need to talk to those men at the bar about something," she said.

"About what?"

"Just go stand by the door . . . and be ready if it's needed." I dared not ask: Ready for what?

Phil walked to the bar and stood behind the biggest and loudest of the beer-swilling patrons. She tapped the large man on the shoulder. He stood almost a head taller than Phil when he turned around. His face was sunburned below his cap that was pushed back on his balding head.

The men's laughter and the conversations stopped. I listened closely from my assigned post near the door.

"What can I do for you, little lady?" the man said, leaning on both elbows against the bar. "Wanna dance with me when the band comes back?" His friends chuckled.

"*Bonsoir, monsieur,*" Phil said. "Could I hear your *blague* again, *s'il te plaît?*"

The big man looked at his friends and then at Phil.

"Come again with that?"

"I did not hear all your fun-fun . . . your *blague* . . . your, how you say, joke," Phil said in a more pronounced accent than I had ever heard her use. "Can you *répéter* for *moi?*"

The man looked at his friends and took a gulp from his tall glass of beer.

"Why sure, little missy. Anything for a cute bug like you," he said, winking at his friends. He attempted to pull his pants up over his belly.

"Okay . . . now listen close, little lady. What's the way to remember how to spell assassination?"

Phil slowly shook her head. The man paused for effect. The men at the bar waited for the punchline.

"It always takes two asses to start it." The big man laughed. His inebriated buddies guffawed.

"*Merci beaucoup* . . . that's what I thought I *entendu.*"

Phil turned slightly toward me, making sure I was in my appointed place. With that, she cocked her right leg behind her like she was getting ready to jump from the dock onto her father's boat. With all the force in her tight and muscular body, she kicked the big man between the legs. The man's friends froze at the bar as the joke-teller yelled in agony and crumbled to the floor. If she had been a place-kicker, the football would have sailed through the goalposts.

"Go," Phil yelled as she ran toward me. I opened the door and followed in an all-out sprint.

"Get your keys out," she yelled, without looking back at me. Instead of opening the car door, she leaped into the passenger's seat of the little convertible in one fluid motion.

I couldn't match Phil's dexterity. As I opened the driver's door in a fumbled panic, I glanced to see one of the bar patrons coming fast at me. I pushed the key in the ignition, but before I could crank the car, a big hand clamped down on my left shoulder and a hairy arm gripped my neck in a headlock. I thought I saw Phil ducking out of the way, but she was reaching underneath my seat. She found my special coffee holder with the heavy lead base and the coat-hanger wires sticking out of it. She slammed the wire prongs into the man's right arm to another cry of pain. The man backed away, cursing and staring at the strange device sticking in his arm. Blood had begun to trickle out around the wires. I started the engine and shot out of the parking lot, gravel flying. My first thought as I got on the lakefront road was that I was glad my license plate light was not working. Yet another repair I had failed to make on my car.

Underpowered as it was, the little sports car took the curves of the lakefront road with no problem. I watched the rear-view mirror. Not seeing any headlights following, I pulled off the main lake road in favor of the back roads. I knew most of them well from my family summers at the lake. The quickest way back to Coldwater was on Highway 61, but I stayed on the less-travelled county roads.

The night air was chilly with the top down. I stopped on the side of the dark road to put up the top.

"I may have broken that guy's coccyx," Phil said, when I got back in the car.

"His what?"

"His coccyx." Phil said. "You know, his tailbone."

"How do you kn-kn-know to call it that?"

"I'll soon be a licensed EMT," she said. "Remember how you and Daddy kept after me to go to school. Well, it took. I know a lot about the parts of the human body and how it works."

Phil brought her right leg up to her chin, gingerly taking off her shoe.

"Speaking of bones, I think I may have broken the metatarsal in my big toe," she said. "Not the first time. I dropped an outboard on it when I was fifteen. I'll know in the morning after the swelling goes down if it's actually broken."

The county roads in Mississippi had no illumination, except for the occasional lighted billboard. I drove in silence, replaying the events at Conway's in my head. I could hear the cries of pain from the two men, but what I remembered with the most detail was dancing with Phil. The violence of the night was no match for the serenity of the dance.

The sign pointed toward Arkabutla Dam.

"I bet that guy will think twice b-b-before he tells that stupid joke again," I said, thinking my statement surely would bring a positive response from Phil, but when I glanced over, she was fast asleep with her dark curls holding steady against the wind.

I drove back to Nellie's in luscious silence, alone with my thoughts about the exciting new plans that I could feel coming together on their own. They tumbled around deep inside me in a space where the worry-haints did not operate. I had never thought about what it meant to "love" somebody. I never ended my letters to Phil with that four-letter word that felt like it was off-limits to me.

190

Phil's visit over the long weekend had started as a simple invitation to a party, but the past forty-eight hours, even with the flare-ups of anger, had opened a new path in front of me. A path that I would ask Phil to walk with me. I had another day to fine tune everything. Phil was good at surprising me, but she had no idea of what life adventure I had in store for her.

CHAPTER II

April 7, 1968
Sunday

ANGELS SINGING in a heavenly choir?

After a deep sleep, getting my morning bearings could prove a challenge. I raised up from my pallet of well-worn quilts, trying to bring everything into focus.

Nellie was quietly singing one of the hymns that I remembered from her time with me in Memphis. She was standing at the stove with an apron on over her solid black dress with a white collar. Blythe, humming the song in a likeable but off-key harmony, was at the table making squares out of knives, forks and spoons. She caught me watching her.

"These are my pens for my chickens," she explained. She put the small salt and pepper shakers shaped liked chickens sitting on nests inside the squares.

"Bernice bought those shakers for us at a five-and-dime in Memphis," Nellie said, without turning around. Sausage patties sizzled and popped on the stove.

I had been too tired to keep the fire going in the woodstove when Phil and I returned to Nellie's around midnight. Phil didn't want to wake Nellie and Blythe by going into the bedroom to change clothes, so she laid down on the couch in the dress she had worn all day. I rested on the pallet that Nellie had readied for me and was thinking about moving it closer to the couch and inviting Phil to join me, but I fell asleep before I could come up with words that sounded proper. It had been a long day and the night had ended in a haze of fury. I still had the image in my head of the man writhing on the floor after Phil kicked her definitive field goal.

Phil turned towards me from the sofa. Her eyes opened, clear and bright.

"How's the toe?" I asked.

"Still swoll up like a balloon, but I don't think it's broken. I tried to move it in the night as much as I could."

Nellie put a plate on the table piled with scrambled eggs and four pieces of sausage the size of hamburger patties.

"Miss Blythe and I are going to go ahead and eat so we can get on to church this morning," Nellie said. "We only got a tiny church, but our Reverend Lucien tends his flock well and his wife can play that old piano long and loud."

As I folded the pallet quilts, Nellie explained that the U.S. Corps of Engineers had constructed the building that her church met in as an office in the 1940s when the dam and levee system were being built. The Corps had deeded the building over to the church in the early 1960s for one dollar. The reverend was a retired Continental Trailways bus driver from Clarksdale, Mississippi. Nellie said the church barely paid him more than the gas money it took to drive from Clarksdale three times a week.

"I know you young'uns got in late last night, but you're welcome to join us for church if you've a mind to," Nellie said.

I turned to Phil for the answer.

"I'd like that, sure" Phil said, "but I slept in the only church-going clothes I have with me."

"God don't pay no mind to wrinkles," Nellie said. "We walk over early for Sunday school, but you can come for big church later if that suits you."

"I don't remember seeing a church around here," I said.

"It's a little walk, but Miss Blythe and I take a back way. It's not that far through the fields."

I told Nellie I could drive them, but it would have to be one at a time because my car was only a two-seater. Nellie insisted they liked the walk so Blythe could pick wildflowers. Phil sat up on the couch and looked down at her right foot. "I stubbed my toe last night and it's still a little sore," she said to Nellie. "I'd like to walk with you, but I may need to ride over in the car."

"That'll be fine," Nellie said, "If you want me to press that dress a little for you, I have time before we leave."

"Oh, no," Phil said. "Just tell me where the iron is and I can do it."

Nellie gave me directions to her church as she washed the breakfast dishes that she and Blythe had used. I noticed there was a sausage patty left on the plate with the eggs.

"Somebody didn't eat their sausage," I said.

"That one is for you and Miss Phil to split," Nellie said. "Miss Blythe don't eat sausage."

"Pigs die when they give sausage. Chickens don't die when they give eggs," Blythe said. The best that both Phil and I could do with that exacting statement was smile and nod.

"Miss Blythe likes the little pigs she sees around as much as she likes her chickens," Nellie said.

Nellie went to her bedroom and came out wearing a small round black hat. Her familiar Bible was in her hands.

"Did you add your day number to your Bible?" I asked Nellie.

"You know I did. First thing of a morning," she said.

"Time for us to be going," Nellie said to Blythe, handing her a small blue bottle. "Here's something to put your flowers in."

"We'll be sure to lock the house," I told Nellie.

"Nothing to lock 'round here," Nellie called from the porch without looking back. "Anybody needs anything I got, they's welcome to it."

PHIL AND I ate breakfast without much conversation. I replayed the previous night's violent events in my head and then erased them with the closeness I felt to Phil on the dance floor.

"I found out Nellie is 78 years old," I said. "She keeps c-c-count of the days she's been alive in her Bible."

I hoped I might get some type of credit for my discovery. I got none. Phil seemed consumed by her own thoughts, much like the state I had been in the night before in the car on our way back to Nellie's. I quickly checked in with those thoughts. They were still percolating nicely.

Phil looked at me between bites of eggs and sausage with that eerie focus that I found both frightening and exciting. There was something she wanted to tell me, but I knew better than to inquire about it. Could it be that my most private and serious thoughts and grand plans had telepathically made their way over from pallet to sofa during the night?

Phil would let me know, but only when she was good and ready.

After we washed and dried our breakfast dishes, Phil went into the bedroom and changed into her flannel pajamas. She set up the spindly ironing board that Nellie kept behind the door.

"Go get me a clean dish cloth from underneath the kitchen sink and sprinkle some water on it from the tap," she said. I obeyed her orders. When I handed the wet cloth to her, she gave me her chastising look.

"Don't you know what 'sprinkle' means?" she said. She took the cloth over to the bowl on Nellie's dresser and wrung out the excess water.

"I guess you don't know," she said, "since you've never had to iron anything."
She covered her dress with the damp cloth and pressed it.

"Take off your pants and shirt and let me touch them up," Phil said after she carefully laid her dress out on Nellie's bed.

"I don't have anything to put on," I said.

"As long as you got underpants on, I'm good," Phil said. "Sit by the heater so you don't get a chill."

Phil handled an iron as well as Nellie. I was content to watch her from a chair I had pulled up next to the small space heater.

"I'm glad Nellie asked us to come to her church," Phil said. "After that *couillon* stunt I pulled last night, I probably need to spend some time in a house of the Lord."

I told Phil I had seen that calm look on her face when she told me to go stand by the door, and that it was the same look she had when she pulled me out of the Mississippi River and patched the large gash on my head after the fall from her skiff.

"Daddy says I get that hard look when I'm ready to set the hook in a yellowfin," Phil said. "I guess that's what it is. My mind takes it upon itself to block out everything except what is there in front of me."

"I know why you kicked that guy, but how did you plan it so well?"

"Not any planning to it," Phil said. "It came to me that it needed to be done . . . and I just did it. Same with that guy that had you around the neck. Had you rather I let him yank you out of the car by the throat?"

"No complaints. I just wish I was as sp-sp-spontaneous and as sure of myself as you." The words turned sour as they came out of my mouth. I had learned nothing from yesterday about being true to who you are and not trying to take on the traits of others.

Phil evidently was feeling charitable. "I could probably take a lesson from you to think things out before I act," Phil said. "In the end, we are who we are. *C'est la vie.*"

Phil handed me my newly pressed pants and shirt.

"Take yourself out of here now and shut the door while I put my dress on," Phil said.

As I had watched her at the ironing, board, I could not get the thought out of my mind that this might be my chance to catch a glimpse of the little *fleur-de-lis* tattoo in the middle of Phil's lower back. The one I had not seen in three years and the image I found myself staring at on the spines of books at the school library. But I knew to follow Phil's orders.

NELLIE'S CHURCH was affiliated with the African Methodist Episcopal Church, the same denomination of the church she belonged to in Memphis. I had asked her what A.M.E. stood for when I went with her to choir practice on Sunday nights when my parents were out of town.

I remembered the heavy-set choir leader from her Memphis church as he put the singers through their paces. He kept a towel draped around his neck to wipe away the perspiration as he jumped around and gave instructions to the choir. I found myself singing and clapping along with the choir and proudly told Nellie that I didn't stutter when I sang. "God don't ever hear no stutters, anyway," she had told me. I thought about that for the next few years when I had a bad day reading aloud in class or answering a question for a teacher. Eventually, I let the thought go. God might not hear them, but everybody else did.

A dozen or so cars were parked in random fashion in the grass around the non-descript cement block building with a flat roof. No steeple. Small casement windows on the sides of the building were fitted with an opaque glass.

"Arkabutla A.M.E. Church" was hand-lettered in black paint above the front door. A small cross made of hammered metal hung above the name. Phil and I heard a piano and a hymn being sung as we opened the solid wooden door. A congregation of three dozen or so sat on wooden benches without backs. The lack of large windows had necessitated the use of harsh fluorescent lighting like you find in most offices. Nellie and Blythe sat on a bench in the second row. Nellie stood and waved for us to come to the front and sit with her, but I pointed that we would take a seat in the back. Besides Blythe, we were the only white people in the church.

The clapping of the churchgoers as they sang and the aggressive piano playing bounced off the concrete-block walls of the small building. The piano was on wheels, and every now and then Reverend Lucien had to scotch the wheels with small blocks of wood to keep it from rolling away as his wife bounced on her stool and hammered the keys. The building had not been constructed with a church in mind, but there was no doubt about the legitimacy of the congregation and what was going on there.

When Reverend Lucien rose for the sermon in his dark suit, the silence was immediate. He strode to the crude lectern deliberately. An oscillating fan on a stand behind the preacher stirred the air slightly, pushing his words toward the congregation.

"Our hearts are heavy this morning . . . but this is where we all need to be gathered . . . in God's place as he looks down on us." The preacher spoke in a hesitating rhythm. Several in the congregation responded with muffled "amens" at the end of his sing-song phrases.

"Before I begin, I believe Sister Avant has some visitors we would like her to introduce us to," Reverend Lucien said. "We all know Miss Blythe here, but who are the two we need to welcome in the back there, Sister Avant?"

Nellie stood and motioned for us to do the same. Sitting on a back bench, isolated, didn't seem like such a good idea all of a sudden.

"Brothers and Sisters, this is my friend from Memphis . . . Vic . . . who I have known since he was just a little man," Nellie said. The pride in her voice was resolute.

"He's now at his college and came for a visit. And this is my new friend, Miss Philomene from down in Louisiana. Ain't she the right pretty one?"

The congregation applauded. Phil clasped her hands in front of her and bowed slightly. I managed a timid smile.

"Welcome to you, Brother and Sister," the preacher said. "You will find our church is humble and small, but our faith is mighty."

Reverend Lucien opened his Bible on the lectern and took out what looked to be a folded page from a newspaper. The congregation watched intently as he spread the page over his Bible and stared at it. His demeanor was calculated and full of emotion. He took a handkerchief from his back pocket and wiped his brow. The congregation waited patiently as the silence and tension built.

"The weight on my heart has been so heavy this week that preparation of a sermon was nigh to impossible," he said. "But I have before me what may be the best sermon ever preached by a mere mortal. Another Sermon on the Mount for all of us to hear and cherish. It was preached Wednesday night at the Mason Temple in Memphis, the headquarters of the Church of God in Christ. And this is what I will read to you this morning for our sermon. Our perfect sermon."

Another dramatic pause.

"I will ask you to put down your fans and cuddle your young'uns for these beautiful words from the late Dr. Martin Luther King." He began to read slowly, pronouncing each word so distinctly that I could almost see them in print.

Something is happening in Memphis. Something is happening in our world.

I had read portions of Dr. King's final speech on the news wires, but the reverend's reading made the words come alive. Dr. King was described on the TV news shows as the master of inflection and Reverend Lucien wasn't far behind. He took the clipping and moved from side to side of the lectern as he read. I strained but was not able to see what newspaper it might have come from. The copy of the speech I had seen transmitted on the Teletype machines was lengthy. One wire story said that Dr. King had spoken that night for more than 20 minutes without any notes. Reverend Lucien's congregation listened in focused silence, only interrupting the sacred mood with quiet "amens." Near the conclusion, the reverend paused.

"Now, congregation, may these last words of our Dr. King burn with a mighty fire in our hearts."

Well, I don't know what will happen now. We've got some difficult days ahead. But it really doesn't matter with me now, because I've been to the mountaintop. And . . . I don't mind.

Like anybody, I would like to live a long life. Longevity has its place. But I'm not concerned about that now. I just want to do God's will. And He's allowed me to go up to the mountain. And I've looked over. And I've seen the Promised Land. I may not get there with you. But I want you to know tonight, that we, as a people, will get to the Promised Land!

And so I'm happy, tonight.

I'm not worried about anything.

I'm not fearing any man.

Mine eyes have seen the glory of the coming of the Lord.

Reverend Lucien put both hands on the lectern and bowed his head. He reached in his back pocket for his handkerchief, wiped the sweat from his brow and then the tears from his eyes.

I realized that Phil and I were holding hands, not knowing which one of us had reached for the other. The congregation, which had been in a reverent stupor, began to clap and shout hallelujahs as the reverend's wife made her way to the piano.

"Please rise," Reverend Lucien said. "We shall now sing Dr. King's favorite hymn, "Take My Hand, Precious Lord.""

My mother had purchased a Christmas album years ago that had Elvis singing that song, but I had never heard it in church.

Nellie sang as loudly as those around her but did not join in the demonstrable waving of the hands and shouting. Nellie had never been one given over to shows of emotion, and it seemed that extended to her worship as well.

Blythe, holding her blue bottle of wildflowers, turned and smiled at us. Phil squeezed my hand. The genuineness of Blythe's smile spoke as loudly to me as the words of the hymn reverberating off the church's concrete block walls.

CHAPTER 12

NELLIE AND BLYTHE had arrived home from church ahead of us even though they had to walk more than a mile through the Delta fields protected by the levee.

I had told Nellie after the service that I wanted to drive somewhere to find a copy of the Sunday newspaper. Phil talked Nellie into not preparing a meal, saying she wanted a hamburger and that we would bring lunch home for everybody. Phil had made sure that I understood she was not comfortable with Nellie cooking for us.

"What can we get that Blythe will eat?" Phil had asked Nellie.

"Don't worry 'bout that. I can fix her a little something." Nellie said, "but it might not hurt if you could find a little cup of vanilla cream for her." Nellie winked at Phil. "But just one dollop. Her mama and daddy say she's not to have too many sweets."

I found a *Commercial Appeal* box in Clarksdale across the highway from a hamburger stand where Phil was ordering our lunch at the window. She hopped over to a bench, stretched out her right leg and took off her shoe, inspecting and then massaging her right toe with both hands.

The play headline in the newspaper was three lines stripped across the top of the page, an unusual layout for the staid morning newspaper:

New Waves Of Violence Erupting

In Chicago, Washington, Pittsburgh;

LBJ Postpones Speech to Congress

A local story lower on the page reported that even though the fire bombings and other violence in Memphis were decreasing, the 7 p.m. to 3 a.m. curfew would remain in effect at least through Monday. Another story on the assassination said that federal authorities were looking for a definite suspect now, but no name was given. The hunt was still on in the area for the elusive white Mustang.

A smaller story on the front page said that 30,000 people were expected to take part in a protest march on Monday in Memphis from Clayborn Temple A.M.E. Church down Main Street and back. The federal district court had approved the plans after Black leaders vowed to the city's leaders that the march would be peaceful.

Monday was going to be busy at the paper, but I was looking forward to it in a way. The work would help ease the pain of putting Phil back on the City of New Orleans that would take her away from me. Then I thought of the plan that was sorting itself out in bits and pieces deep inside me. I longed to be at a typewriter to put down the exact words I might say to Phil, and as I thought of the words, I had to ball my hands up into fists to keep them from shaking with excitement.

AFTER WE FINISHED LUNCH, I turned through the Sunday newspaper on Nellie's porch. The stories I was pretending to read didn't register with me.

Phil had asked Nellie to show her how she created her needle stories. Nellie sat on the couch inside between Phil and Blythe, talking as she sewed her colored threads in and out of the cloth. Blythe ate the last of her ice cream cup. I could hear their conversation through the screen door.

"I know how you see to put the needle in from the front, but how can you tell from the back without turning it over and looking?" Phil asked.

"I don't rightly know," Nellie said. "I reckon the story just tells the needle where to go. I don't think about it much. I just think about the story."

"I can hear the needle tell the story to the cloth," Blythe said, licking the ice cream from a small wooden spoon. "Miss Nellie's needles can talk like my chickens."

Nellie was correct. I was beginning to understand and enjoy Blythe's observations.

The large black Cadillac turned off the gravel road into the yard. I stepped off the porch to meet it. The Black driver, this time not wearing a tie with his suit coat, exited the car.

"Here to collect Miss Blythe," the driver said.

"Good Sunday to you, Mr. Randall," Nellie said, walking onto the porch. "I told Miss Blythe to gather up her things when I heard you coming. She'll be out in a minute." Nellie came down the steps.

"This is my friend from long ago in Memphis," Nellie said.

The driver reached out his hand. "Please to meet you, sir. I'm Randall Pease."

"Vic," I said as I shook his hand, surprising myself when I was able to say my first name cleanly without the familiar glottal block.

"Things okay in Memphis with Blythe's family's business?" Nellie asked Randall.

"We just got back a whilst ago," Randall said. "I don't think the office on Front Street was bothered and the cotton warehouses out by the train yards are hard for anybody to mess with."

Phil and Blythe came out through the screen door together. Blythe set a small suitcase down on the steps and took off running around the house. Phil sat down on the steps.

"Be quick, Miss Blythe. Mr. Randall is waiting on you," Nellie said.

"She's saying goodbye to the chickens," Nellie explained to Randall.

An uncontrollable urge came over me. I wanted to talk to Randall, a stranger. Not with perfunctory words but a true conversation.

"Do you find it s-s-safe driving in Memphis in times such as these?" I asked.

"Not much more than usual," Randall said. "Us country folks know to have our city eyes on when we're in Memphis."

City eyes? Superficially, I understood.

"Did you grow up around here?" I asked.

"Born and raised in Kosciusko 'bout two hours south of here but had to come to Memphis to find a job," he said. "Been working for Miss Blythe's daddy at the cotton company going on twenty years."

Randall was easy to talk to. More questions welled up inside me.

Blythe soon came back around the house. When she reached for her small case on the front steps, Phil grabbed her hands and pulled her down to sit.

"Miss Blythe, it was so nice to meet you, sure, and I hope we can see each other again one day," Phil said.

Blythe smiled. "Me too."

She paused, looking hard into Phil's eyes, and then said, "I like the way you say "sure" all the time. It makes me happy."

I found myself walking toward Blythe and Phil, words piling up in my head but without a notion of how they might come out; just knowing I needed to give it my best effort. My knee crunched and popped as I knelt in front of Blythe and next to Phil.

"Take care of Nellie and the chickens . . . and I'll be around to help . . . if you need me," I said, relieved that my words came out without large gaps, and more importantly, that my intentions seemed to make sense in that moment.

Blythe stared at me. "Minnie. Mary. Martha. Margaret. Maggie. Missy," she said.

"I won't forget their names," I said.

Randall opened the rear door of the Cadillac for Blythe. The car turned around in the yard and eased onto the gravel road. I wanted to tell both Nellie and Phil that I was genuinely sorry to see Blythe and Randall go, but the words didn't seem necessary.

THE WARMING AFTERNOON lay in front of me as the three of us sat on the front porch. We were less than one hour from Memphis, from campus, from the newspaper, but that world seemed far away, underneath the shadow of a quiet Mississippi River levee.

My intuition had been working overtime and my intellect was trying to catch up. I wanted to talk with Nellie and Phil together, and then have that important conversation only with Phil that had been working itself out inside of me. How could I make that happen? Phil would tell me to "get on with the gettin' on."

I did, crashing in on the subject at hand without any introductory warnings.

"Nellie, did you know that my father was not my b-b-biological father . . . you know . . . not the man who made me with my mother?"

Nellie did not shock easily. She sat on her ladderback chair on the porch. Phil had her right shoe off and was sitting on the wooden stoop.

"Not for a known fact, but I reckon I had some sense of it," Nellie said. "Mr. V was tall and thin, and you don't much take after him in your looks and your ways."

I let her words sink in.

"Your daddy had the prettiest blue eyes," Nellie continued. "And your eyes are pretty but they as brown as the water in Coldwater Creek." I regretted not paying more attention to the eye-color chapter in high school biology.

I explained to both Phil and Nellie how I had found my birth certificate when I was 11 years old that said my father was "unknown," but I never had the courage to say anything until I returned from my trip to Louisiana and my parents told me they were going to be getting a divorce.

"Did you talk to Mrs. V about it?" Nellie asked.

"She said that the b-b-birth certificate was just a 'clergical error' and that certainly my father was my only father . . . and that she didn't want to talk about such foolishness anymore. I guess she meant 'clerical error'," I said, trying to add a small laugh.

"What about Mr. V? Did you talk to him?"

"All he said was that as far he was c-c-concerned, he was my rightful father."

Phil broke in. "So, what does that mean exactly?"

"I think he was trying to tell me that he knew he was not my b-b-biological father and that he had known it all along and was okay with it."

Nellie broke in. "I would say that's 'bout right, Vic. Your daddy was a good man, and you couldn't have had a better soul taking care of you. Any man can make a child, but a daddy is one who raises that child and sees to it that the boy he calls his son has a good start."

I had more to the story and wanted the words to come out.

"I found out later on from my father's s-s-sister that he had rheumatic fever when he was a kid and the doctor told the family how he might not be able to have children," I explained. "My aunt said the family had always thought of me as the 'miracle baby.' "

"*Miracles* happen every night some place on this earth," Phil said. The French pronunciation of the word added to its meaning.

"Don't be worrying about some other man making you," Phil continued. "You are who you are. Don't matter who you came from. What matters is what you make of your own self. In the end, we all have to make our own way."
Phil put her shoe on, came up on the porch and sat on the floor in front of me.

"You met my daddy," she said. "There's not a calmer and more respected boat captain in South Louisiana. And look at me. His *couillon* daughter, who can't keep her smart mouth at anchor."

She wasn't done.

"You keep looking for someone to tell you who you are and what you should be about, but you get to decide that for yourself. I can almost see it as a blessing, sure."

I looked to Nellie for understanding.

"What Miss Philomene is saying is that you came from God and that's all that needs to be weighed. Your momma and daddy both made sure you had a good start and you need to keep it going now that you are more on your own."

Phil nodded. "You said it better, Nellie. Thank you."

Another one of my worry-haints that had chased me for a decade had been exposed in a few minutes of conversation with two people that I loved the most. Loved in different ways but with no less intensity.

And *love* was at the center of the conversation I wanted to have alone with Phil.

I had been thinking carefully about the words I would use, ever since I knew Phil was coming to Memphis, but the weekend had brought a new urgency to my plans, taking me to places I didn't know I would be going. I knew what I needed to talk to Phil about now, and it felt good and so right in the rush of the weekend that was flowing uncontrolled like the current of the nearby Mississippi River.

EVEN IN THE CRISPNESS of spring, breezes that came from the Arkansas side of the river brought humidity with them. Phil had assured me she could make it to the top of the levee on her sore toe. The exercise would help keep it from tightening up, she said.

We had borrowed an old blanket from Nellie to sit on. Phil was in a talkative mood and chatting as we sat down, possibly proud of me that I had raised the issue of my father. Phil eased off the shoe on her right foot. The big toe had turned several shades of black and blue, but she could wiggle it.

"You know, I'm glad we went to Nellie's church this morning," Phil said. "I liked that the preacher read Dr. King's speech. I loved every word and it was good to hear it in Nellie's church." I agreed.

"But I've got a confession to make, and I'll probably need to make it official with my priest when I get back to Louisiana," Phil said.

"What confession?"

"Well, with all that talk about non-violence and turning the other cheek, all I can think about is that I'm not sorry that I let that guy at the bar have it good, sure. Instead of turning a cheek, I made *positif* that guy felt it right between his cheeks."

I didn't know if I should laugh, but Phil's smile gave me the go ahead.

"I do hope the man's not hurt in any kind of a permanent way," Phil continued, "but he had no right to make that terrible joke and without *sanction*."

"I don't know your Catholic rules well, but my guess would be that skipping that confession won't get you in any trouble."

"I think that other man that had you 'round the neck wasn't hurt too bad," Phil said. "I didn't jab as hard as I could have with your coffee holder, but I'd say it got his *attention*, sure."

Phil and I laid back on the blanket. I watched the lazy clouds, trying to find my courage to get on with my gettin' on.

"Phil, I've been doing a lot of thinking and I've come up with something that I want to talk with you about . . . s-s-seriously," I said, as I turned to face her on the blanket. "I don't have it all figured out . . . but I know enough to start us out . . . and I know we can make it work . . . together."

Most plans sounded good as long as they stayed in my head but usually started to crumble as soon as I found a way to voice them, but these words I had stored up came out in a good stream and grew more thrilling the longer I stuck with them. For once, the worry-haints kept their distance in the background.

I started out explaining that my plan was to talk to Chis about a full-time and paid internship at the paper starting in June, only two months away. Chis was in charge of interns, and I had a good chance of getting a spot. Phil would be finished with her two-year degree at about the same time. If she could get an EMT job in Memphis and I got the paid internship, we could find a small apartment in Memphis and have plenty to live on. We could save our money and after a few years, she could get her four-year degree and I would do something about finishing mine at another college. My father would still be good for the tuition, but my plans would give him a little breathing room without that tuition expense hanging over his head. I had some good paychecks coming from all the overtime I had been working and there probably would be more in the coming weeks with all the news that was breaking. We could visit Nellie on the weekends and take some longer weekends and go visit Phil's family in Louisiana. I might even have some money left to get my car back in good repair.

And then the clincher.

"When we b-b-both feel it's the right time, we can . . . you know . . . go to Louisiana and get a license and get married," I said. "I've never b-b-been to a Catholic wedding, but I'll make it through the v-v-vows somehow."

I had hoped my little joke and the stutter that somehow seemed appropriate would warrant a response. Nothing from Phil. She was usually good about looking at me when I talked to her, but now her head was rigid as she stared at the sky.

"Of course, we could just get m-m-married by a judge," I said, trying to fill the silence. "Judges do that all the time in Memphis . . . and I know where their courtrooms are . . . and you can have any kind of wedding you want . . . and . . . ." I continued to ramble. I was so nervous about the words that were coming out that I forgot to be concerned about my stutter.

Phil got up from the blanket and put on her shoe. I turned on my knees to join her.

"Stay here, Vic," Phil said in her stern ship-captain's voice. "I need to walk for a minute."

"I'll walk with you," I said, ignoring Phil's order and vowing not to let her put the brake on all that was inside me and ready to spill out.

"I mean what I say, Vic. You need to stay right here. Just let me walk a little and collect my thoughts."

"Look, I didn't mean to sp-sp-spring that on you so fast, but I know now it's what I want to do. It's what we need to do, and . . . ."

Phil raised her hand to give the order for me to stop talking. Her resolute calmness had taken over again. I could imagine her reeling in a large tuna, outrunning a hurricane on the river in her tiny skiff, sending a large man to the floor with a swift kick.

I SAT ALONE on the blanket. Was Phil considering my proposal I had sprung on her so clumsily. No. My intuition told me my plans were being swept over the levee and into the swirling waters of the Mississippi River. I was missing something, and I had no clue what it was. I had no inkling of what I had done to cause Phil to want to move away from me, both physically and emotionally.

Phil walked toward the end of the levee. She sat down in a patch of Forget-Me-Nots. The flowers no longer reached for the sun. They had begun to wilt in the heat, which was starting to get its legs again in the Mississippi delta. I watched her as long as I dared and then turned over on my stomach on the blanket and closed my eyes. The worry-haints were back and stomping me down into the packed red dirt of the levee.

I BRUSHED SOMETHING off the back of my head and turned to see Phil standing over me, letting wilted Forget-Me-Nots drop from her hand, exactly as Blythe had done. I sat up.

"Welcome b-b-back," I said. "I think."

Phil's impenetrable calmness remained, but was accompanied by a determined smile, which made the moment bearable. She sat down next to me on the blanket and began.

"I have called you names. I have accused you of being selfish and of not being truthful when it was me who has been the most selfish and untruthful," she said. "I have something to tell you, Vic, and we both are going to hurt. I . . . ."

I spun and jumped to my feet. I didn't have to plan my words. I spoke loudly, not because it helped me not to stutter but because the words had their own volume, force and urgency. She was calm, but I let my anger have its head. I let go. The words came out in a gush. No brakes anywhere.

"If you're getting ready to tell me about somebody else, about another . . . another man, you can just forget it. We have not seen each other in three years, and you didn't give me a chance except for reading all my stupid letters . . . which I know now I shouldn't have written. You have reasons not to have any confidence in me, but I can change. I can make you a good . . . a good husband. I love you, Phil. You have to understand that. I can take care of you . . . I mean . . . I know you don't need taking care of, but don't let some other man get in our way. I don't know who it is, but I love you better than he does. I . . . I *garantie*."

I closed my eyes at my idiotic Cajun-French pronunciation of "guarantee" that came out of nowhere. And why did I have to say I would take care of somebody who needed no taking care of? A fool's words if I ever heard them, but words I had no choice but to say. I had never told anyone that I "loved" them. The word should have felt good and satisfying. It was neither.

I didn't want to hear what Phil had to say. I turned and walked, then ran on my aching knee in the direction Phil had come from. I trampled her patch of wilting Forget-Me-Nots. I ran until the levee started sloping to its termination. My erratic thoughts turned to the night before in Conway's. If Phil thought she could kick, she hadn't seen anything yet. I was the place-kicker for my high school's football team before I blew out my knee. Show me Phil's new boyfriend or manfriend and I'll show him what a long field goal feels like right between the . . . .

It was my fault. I should have made my way down to Louisiana again to see Phil, but all I did was write stupid letters. I only talked about myself in the letters. I never told her how much I loved her.

Just like I never said the things I should have said to Nellie. I sprung my crude marriage proposal on Phil like the fool I was. I was sure my Intellect and Intuition were going to come together in my grand plan, but all that happened was that Mr. Spiro's two I-Powers exploded in my face.

The clouds had cleared the way for the sun to start its descent on the Arkansas horizon. Dark comes quickly on a levee. I could barely make out Phil in the distance sitting on the blanket. I started back. Empty and with the worry-haints nipping at me with every step. I approached carefully.

"Have you calmed down?" Phil asked.

I shook my head. "Not really. I d-d-don't understand how you could do this to me. How you could . . . ."

Phil's louder than normal voice interrupted me. "Just sit down and be quiet a minute and let me talk. It's not what you think. You have every right to be upset with me, but it's not for the reason you have conjured up."

Phil's voice maintained its calm cadence.

"I'll be finished with EMT school around the middle of May," she explained. "And I've already enlisted in the U.S. Navy on a five-year commitment to be a Hospital Corpsman."

How could she have done this with telling me? *ME.* I wanted to rage at her with the question, but—for once—hitting the brakes came in handy. As much as I desired it to be, this might not be about me.

"I took the Armed Services Vocational Aptitude test and passed with good marks," she continued. No congratulations from me.

"I report to Fort Sam Houston on May 21 for 19 weeks of training. Because of my EMT cert and five-year signup, I'll be an officer when I finish my training in Texas."

There it was. Her next five years laid out in a nice to-do list. A to-do list that had nothing to do with me.

"What happens then?" I asked. I hated that the question came out sounding as if I had already lost and given in.

"Most likely Vietnam," she said without emotion.

"But I thought you hated the war," I said. "I thought you were against it."

"I do. I am against it," she said. "But I'm gonna be helping people. Not fighting or killing. You might could say I'm almost protesting in my own *couillon* way."

"Did your uncle talk you into this?" I asked. I had met her mother's brother, Gene, briefly in Louisiana. He had been a Navy Hospital Corpsman and I knew Phil was fond of him. Gene was the one who had stitched up the gash in my head after Phil got me off the river and before the hurricane hit.

"He doesn't know anything yet," Phil said. "No one in my family knows. You're the only one I've told. I only signed my enlistment papers on Wednesday."

Was I supposed to be proud of that?

"Wednesday? You mean the d-d-day before you got on the train to come up here?" I asked.

Phil nodded. "I was afraid if I didn't sign then, I never would."

"Can you g-g-get out of it, change your mind?" I knew the answer to my fumbling question as soon as I asked it.

"Can't and don't want to," Phil said, "but I need to tell you all the story. There's more to it."

For the next twenty minutes as the darkness swallowed up the levee, Phil told me her story. It could have been summed up in one word. Helicopters.

She had gotten her parttime job fueling and doing simple maintenance on helicopters that ferried supplies and workers to the oil rigs in the Gulf of Mexico. She became friends with the pilots and talked them into giving her rides, even though it was against company policy. Occasionally, she would wrangle a special clearance to make an official flight to an oil rig to check on helicopters there. She explained that most of the pilots would let her take the controls for a portion of the flight. *Collective pitch control. Anti-torque control. Cyclic pitch control.* The phrases rolled off her tongue excitedly. She moved imaginary controls with her hands and feet as she explained with an excited precision how to pilot a helicopter.

I didn't stop her. The fact that I seemed to be losing Phil to something inanimate—a helicopter—was a relief in a strange way. I would never be able to bear the thought that I was losing her to someone else. To another *manboy*.

"But what does flying helicopters have to do with being a Navy corpsman?" I asked, trying to find any leverage, struggling not to admit defeat.

"Women aren't allowed to fly into combat zones," she explained, "but the recruiter I talked with said some women are getting to the front lines as EMTs."

"Does the Navy even let women pilot helicopters?" I asked.

"Not yet," Phil said, "but my sense tells me it won't be long. The Navy flies Bell Iroquois helicopters called 'Hueys.' Most of the oil rig helicopters we fly are made by Bell. If you put me in one of those Hueys right now, I *garantie* I could take off and put you down anywhere you wanted. All right, maybe with a little more practice, but I'm going to be the best MedEvac pilot in the Navy."

I knew the futility of trying to talk Phil out of a plan that she taken great pains to construct, but I had to try something.

"Phil, if you want to p-p-pilot your daddy's boat on charters or keep on flying to oil rigs, I'll move down to Louisiana and you can do that and I can get a job, maybe even on an oil rig. I don't know much about it, but I know the pay is good and I don't mind learning something new. I don't think you've seen me at my strongest . . . at my b-b-best." As I reflected on my words that were coming out of me, they felt laughable. There was something to be said for brakes, but Phil was easy on me.

"I don't doubt you could do it, but you don't belong on an oil rig in the middle of the Gulf, Vic. You belong at a typewriter. Just the same as I know flying MedEvacs is where I belong. I loved the ocean because that's all I knew. The first time I went up in a helicopter, I felt the same freedom that the ocean had given me, but it was multiplied out many times in the air, up above everything."

"But a chopper in Vietnam . . . " Phil put up her hand.

"Never call it a 'chopper.' That's what civilians call them. It's always to be called a 'helicopter.' "

"Okay, but a helicopter in V-V-Vietnam is dangerous. We have stories in the paper all the time about them crashing, even on training flights," I said. "It's just not s-s-safe."

Phil was ready for me.

"It's not safe taking Mr. Spiro's ashes to the Mouth of the Mississippi River," Phil said. "It's not safe standing on the balcony of the Lorraine Motel. If you get down to it, living is not safe, but you do what you know you have to do. And you have to be who you are in order to live your life fully."

I was determined not to let go.

"Okay, if you have to fly helicopters, I'll find the money somehow for you to take private lessons and you can fly out to the oil rigs. I'll get a job and we can live in Louisiana.

Phil shook her head.

"Private lessons are expensive, Vic. Every pilot I know that flies to the rigs is ex-military."

I was out of rebuttals.

"I'm not all that anxious to be going to Vietnam, but I don't see any other way to get into helicopters, and I get to help people by doing it while I'm learning something new," Phil said. "I know I'll be good at it . . . and it's what I know I have to do."

I could not look at her but heard the calmness in her voice waning.

"I feel bad for what I have done to you this weekend. I didn't plan it this way. I was going to tell you as soon as we had a chance to talk. I thought I was doing it right by telling you in person . . . but it came out too late and all wrong. I'm sorry."

I didn't want apologies. I was too numb to be able to want anything.

Student. Servant. Seller. Seeker. The four words came back to me. The four words that Mr. Spiro used to explain his philosophy of the "Quartering of the Soul." I knew that Phil was the embodiment of all four words, and I knew that Mr. Spiro would say that she had the "quartering" exactly right because she chose to live the kind of life that put all four parts in a careful balance.

Mr. Spiro and his last request to spread his ashes at the mouth of the Mississippi River was the reason I met Phil in the first place. Even if he were still alive, I would never be able to thank him enough, even though I could feel her being carried away from me. Far away. In a noisy, air-thumping helicopter, no less.

Chapter 13

OUT OF NECESSITY, we held hands in the near darkness as we walked down from the levee.

Phil's painful toe caused her to limp. She confided that she hoped her foot would heal before her basic training started. She had no trouble letting me know that her enlistment was a done deal. Losing Phil was becoming real, not just a dread from some far-off place filled with haints. I felt guilty in my relief that I was not losing her to someone else, but there was no doubt that she was slipping away from me in a current that I was ill-equipped to deal with, other than to heed Mr. Spiro's advice not to fight it.

Nellie's chickens cackled softly inside the coop as we passed.

"I'd rather we didn't tell Nellie about my Navy plans," Phil said. "You can tell her later on when . . . if . . . you see her again."

"What makes you think I won't be seeing her again?" My tone had a certain aggressiveness to it that I had not intended, but it felt as if I was talking to a different person. Someone now who was never going to be *my girl.*

I waited for a comeback to the order of "well, you ignored her for eight years," but Phil let it go.

"Let's not take our feelings into Nellie's house," Phil said. "I want to remember this house for all the good and kindness that is in it."

I responded with a nod that may have been imperceptible.

"You have every right to be mad at me, Vic, but we shouldn't make Nellie pay the price."

"I'm not mad, Philomene . . . confused, yes . . . but not mad," I heard myself say. I rarely called her by her full name. Phil had become Philomene. I was no longer Sporty Boy.

I waited for her response, but no more words came.

Nellie was in her nightgown and cap as we came in through the backdoor and into the kitchen.

"Law me, I thought them haints had swallowed you up in the dark out there on the levee," she said.

Nellie had been the one who had first taught me about haints years ago in Memphis. If I could only explain to her how well that I knew them now.

"Bernice brought over some light bread whilst you were gone," Nellie said. "I can make you a sandwich of some call."

Phil and I agreed that we weren't hungry. The City of New Orleans would be leaving at six-thirty the next morning from Central Station and we would need to leave Nellie's no later than 5 a.m. We needed to get some sleep. Several weeks prior, I had changed my Monday schedule to start my shift at 8 a.m. instead of 4 a.m. The newsroom would be busy with plenty for me to do. I was glad for that and looking forward to my mindless duties at the newspaper that would keep me busy.

Nellie asked Phil if she wanted her pallet in the bedroom.

"That couch was good last night," Phil said. "I'll just *s'endormir* there."

Nellie smiled at Phil and then at me.

"You two know how God mixed up everybody's words at that Tower of Babel into different ways of talking," Nellie said. "Miss Philomene uses her own Louisiana words, but I can understand her talking just fine. I think God worked it out like that ages ago and it's still working today."

I nodded, wondering what God had to do with taking Phil away from me, but that kind of thinking only served to keep my mind going around in never-ending circles.

PHIL CHANGED into her pajamas in Nellie's bedroom while I went out to my car in the darkness and slipped on a pair of gym shorts from my trunk. Inside, I folded my pants carefully across the back of a chair.

Phil asked Nellie if she would help wash her hair.

"If you don't mind scrap soap," Nellie said. "Let me get us a wash pan and we'll go out on the back stoop. We'll have those pretty curls of yours looking nice when you get home."

I remembered Nellie's "scrap soap" well. She would gather all the small bits of bar soap from the kitchen and the bathrooms at our house, run some hot water over the pile and mold the scraps into bars with her strong hands. The soap bars were multicolored and seemed to grow magically.

I thought about sneaking a peek at Phil with her hair wet once again, like I had seen it when she dived into the Mississippi River for the healing mud to pack on my gashed head. I decided against it, knowing that the moment of pleasure would only cause more pain later.

Phil came back in the front room, ruffling a thin towel through her hair.

"Nellie ground up some small leaves from her lilac bush in the water we washed in," Phil said. "Looks like I won't be smelling like a tush hog when I get home."

The longer she dried her hair, the more the curls came alive. I pretended I was interested in going to sleep on my pallet on the floor. I knew I had to find a way to give up on the thought that Phil was mine. She belonged to the sea. To the air. To the Navy. To helicopters. To something else. She didn't belong to me.

She never had, I decided.

Phil pulled the quilt over her on the couch. I thought about saying "good night," but there was nothing good about it and sleep seemed a ridiculous proposition anyway. I usually started out the night on my stomach, but it felt like a good time to stay on my back and stare at the ceiling, if only to keep an eye on the worry-haints that would be buzzing around me all night.

I felt my face burning with embarrassment in the dark. How stupid of me to suggest that I could pick up and move to Louisiana and work on an oil rig. What idiotic words can come out of a mouth when dreams were threatened. When something was being taken away. Maybe I was destined forever to be that cursed soul known as *manboy*.

There was nothing else to say to say to Phil. Any more conversation on the subject would only make matters worse. The worry-haints had won and they would be celebrating, having a taunting *fais do-do* in my head all night.

PHIL WHISPERED. Her lips were close to my ear.

"Is it too cruel to ask you to hold me?" She had eased down off the couch on to my pallet silently.

I put my arms around her as she backed closer into me. Her pajamas were warm. I could smell Nellie's lilac and the scent of fresh soap in her hair. She spoke quietly.

"Think about how quickly these past three years have gone," Phil said. "Five years will fly by too. We'll both be busy. Doing what we have to do."

I said nothing, even though I liked to whisper to Phil because I rarely stuttered in that voice.

"You can write to me as much as you want, but you need to understand that I probably can't write you back all that much, especially during the first months of training," Phil said. She was trying to make it easier on me. I guess I appreciated that.

I think she felt my nod, but I would not be writing my selfish letters to her. My three years of writing had been for me, not Phil. I was just using her to read my letters, thinking only about myself. It was *manboy* writing of the worst kind and there would be no more of that. I saw clearly where that pathetic and self-absorbed thinking had gotten me.

"Vic, you understand, don't you, that I'm not asking you to wait on me. That's not fair to either one of us. We both have to live each day, on its own for what it is, and just be thankful that, in one way, we will always have each other."

I could only believe this was Phil's way of saying goodbye.

My mind went back to the first day I saw Phil at her parents' house in Louisiana. The day she first called me "Sporty Boy." Our first kiss in the swamp grass of the bayou. The brief glimpse of the *fleur-de-lis* on her back. The haunting—yet wonderful—drive to New Orleans to outrun the hurricane and fulfill Mr. Spiro's wish. Writing her the note on my old typewriter that . . . .

Phil squirmed in my arms.

"Sorry," I whispered as I backed my hips away from her slightly.

"It's all good, Sporty Boy. I understand . . . and I feel the same way, but there's no need to start something that we can't finish."

Her words must have sounded crueler than she had intended because she tacked on something just for my benefit, just to ease the pain. "At least not . . . you know . . . for a while."

Much like I could understand her French and her words in the Cajun dialect so well, I could understand the meaning behind her words "for a while." What she meant was *forever*. At least I got to hear "Sporty Boy" one more time.

I pretended sleep had come again but my thoughts were spinning. I felt my fingers on imaginary keys.

One of the last passages I ever typed when I was wasting time doing all the silly copying was from a book called *To Have and Have Not*. I couldn't remember the words exactly, but I let the memory in my fingers under the quilt tap out the words that went something like *how do you get through nights if you can't sleep? I guess I'm finding out right now. You just go dead inside and everything is easy.*

I had never understood what the title of that book meant, but it was all too clear now. I would always have Phil in one way but would never have her in the way I had hoped. Would I need to go dead inside to make it without her?

I held her carefully in my arms but at a proper distance until the shroud of sleep finally won out over both of us.

CHAPTER 14

April 8, 1968
Monday

A STIRRING came from Nellie's bedroom. The cracked door cast a fractured light into our front room.

At some point during the night, Phil had crawled back onto the couch. She was still asleep, facing away from me. Her pajama top was hiked slightly above her waist. In the meager light I could make out the tattoo about the size of a quarter in the middle of her lower back—the outline of the *fleur-de-lis*. The only other time I had seen it was three years earlier on the banks of a Louisiana bayou after we had chased swamp rabbits and she had asked me to brush off the swamp-grass seeds from her back.

According to Mr. Spiro, the *fleur-de-lis* symbolized life, perfection and light. I had thought about asking her where and when she got the tattoo, maybe even why, but I could hear her telling me that it *was none of my busyness, sure.*

I found my hand reaching for the tattoo, but I then I drew back. The last thing I needed was a repeat of the uncontrollable urge when Phil joined me on the pallet during the night. To have and have not.

The door of the chifforobe in Nellie's bedroom opened with its familiar squeak and then closed.

Phil turned on her back and stretched her arms into the air. "What time is it?" she asked.

I could barely make out the hands on my watch. "I think a little after 4."

"I'll go in Nellie's room and change," Phil said.

Nellie opened her bedroom door all the way.

"I didn't think you two young'uns would be up," she said. "I guess I'm still remembering years back when it took most of a morning for Little Man to come to life. I'll put some coffee on and cook us some of Miss Blythe's eggs."

Nellie put a spoonful of bacon grease in her big iron skillet.

"Ol' Minnie, Mary, Martha, Margaret, Maggie, Missy, been earning their keep," Nellie said and laughed. "Ain't that Miss Blythe something else, naming those chickens like that and talkin' to them like she does?"

Nellie hummed one of her hymns as she cracked two eggs simultaneously in the skillet, one in each hand. Nellie's voice felt like the salve she long ago would put on my skinned knees and elbows.

PHIL HAD CHANGED into the same jeans and t-shirt that she had arrived in four days earlier at Central Station.

"Somebody ironed the wrinkles out of the clothes I had stuffed in my bag," Phil said, smiling at Nellie.
"I thought you might need them freshened up a mite to go back home in," Nellie said.

I took my clothes into Nellie's bedroom and changed quickly. When I came back out, a steaming plate heaped with scrambled eggs was on the table along with pieces of toast. Phil helped herself.

"These eggs have to last me 'til I get back to Louisiana," Phil said. "Those train conductors want to take your last penny with their *scandaleux* prices."

I tried a few bites of eggs, but they weren't going down easy with the emotions from the night that continued to rip through me. The worry-haints even seemed confused as to what to do. I sipped my coffee.

"Sorry I didn't have flapjack makings for you," Nellie said to me. "You and Mr. Rat could sure 'nough eat your way through a stack of 'em. Do you ever see that friend-boy of yours anymore?"

I shook my head. Phil gave me the look that meant for me to step out of my standoffish mood and pick up my conversation.

"We lost touch after our m-m-move to the new house and I changed schools," I explained. "He went out of town to college, and we don't see each other anymore."

"I don't mean to be casting spells, but somehow I never thought that moving to that new house was a good idea for you and your parents," Nellie said. "Peoples move hither and yon, but they carry their own houses with them like a mud turtle. You rightly can't move away from your own self."

Phil saw that I was still too caught up in my emotions to make worthwhile conversation. She pitched in to help me.

"Vic is thinking he might get a good job at the newspaper when he gets out of school," Phil said. "He's working on another newspaper story about a book that helps people find a safe place when they travel."

Phil looked at me to pick up the conversation, but I could only check my watch.

"We n-n-eed to be sure to get to the train on time," I said.

Phil went into the bedroom and came back with her bag, the one with the evil totem of a helicopter on it.

"You travel nice and light, Miss Phil," Nellie said.

"It's the best way to go," Phil said. "I'm so glad I finally got to meet you, Nellie, after Vic told me so much about you."

"I'm glad to get to know you, too," Nellie said. "I just knew Vic would find him a pretty friend-girl like you."

Friend-girl. Nellie had it exactly right. There was a huge difference between a *friend-girl* and a *girlfriend.* I would need to find a way to convince myself that I was lucky to have at least the first one. A challenge I was not looking forward to.

The conversation between Nellie and Phil felt like it was for my benefit; like Nellie already knew that this was the last time she would see Phil; like this was the last time I would see Phil. The worry-haints had gotten their strength back and they bore down on me. I had to make some relief for myself.

"I usually have Sundays and Mondays off . . . and I'll be coming to see you more now that I know exactly where you live," I said to Nellie. "I'll give B-B-Bernice my phone number and she can call me if you ever need anything from Memphis."

Nellie seemed puzzled at my words.

"Not sure what I might be needing from Memphis but you know you're welcome here anytime."

Phil dropped her bag from her shoulder and gave Nellie a two-armed hug that lasted longer than normal. Then Nellie turned to me.

"I'm gonna call you 'Little Man' this one last time and then I'll be done with it," Nellie said. She put her hands on my shoulders, those same strong arms that had pulled me out of that storm drain in front of my house thirteen years ago.

"You have grown up nice and I'm proud of you. I'm glad to know you'll be writing some good things to put in that newspaper of yours." Hearing Nellie say it somehow made it seem possible.

I gave Nellie the same long hug as Phil had and then it shot through me like an assassin's bullet that Phil and I essentially were hugging each other through Nellie's intercession. I felt both sadness and relief in that hug.

"Go on and catch that fast train, now," Nellie said. "I ain't never been on one, but I know they don't wait for nobody."

Fast train? Yes, Nellie understood that it was the train taking Philomene Moreau away from me for the last time.

HIGHWAY 51 didn't give up much conversation. When I finally looked at Phil, tears ran down her face, but no sobs. She had seen my tears in Louisiana on the bridge with Mr. Spiro's ashes, but I had always thought that she was not capable of tears.
Surely there were no tears for me at this late hour. "What's wrong?" I asked.

She opened the shoulder bag she held tightly in her lap. I had wondered why she didn't put the bag in the trunk when we left

Nellie's house. From the top of her bag, she pulled out one of Nellie's needle stories.

"Nellie put this in my bag without telling me," Phil said. "I had told her when I first saw it that it was my favorite."

I recognized the flour-sack cloth and colorful threads that told the story of Moses and the Burning Bush. Nellie had explained to me in her room over the garage in Memphis how the bush was never consumed and that it was a sign from God to Moses that he should lead his people to the Promised Land even though he stuttered and had not recognized his self-worth. The bright red threads leaped from the dark branches of the bush.

I searched for words to try to comfort Phil.

"Mam . . . I mean Nellie . . . never gave me one of her needle stories," I said, immediately realizing how wrong the words sounded and how Phil and I were already losing whatever had connected us in the past.

"Did you ever tell her how much you liked them?" Phil shot back at me.

"Sorry," I said.

"No, I'm sorry. I know you didn't mean it like that," Phil said. "I could tell from your letters how much you loved Nellie, even though you were lacking in ways to show it."

"I know that she gave me much more than I ever thought about giving her," I said. "But I'm going to do b-b-better now." Phil seized on my confessional air.

"Do you understand why I said that you belong at a typewriter and not any place else?" Phil asked.

I did, even though it was hard to admit it to myself.

"You need your words on paper to better figure out how you feel," Phil said. "If you keep putting down your words, those thoughts you need to share with others will come easier for you."

I could only hope she was right because no words were coming now.

WE ARRIVED at the almost empty Central Station parking lot on South Main shortly after 6 a.m.

I had a question for Phil that I had looked at from every angle I could think of as we approached the train station. Questioning Phil was risky, but I took a chance. The words surprised me because they came out without a stutter.

"When did you plan on telling me about enlisting in the Navy?"

"It's the main reason I came to Memphis. I didn't know how or when, but I knew I had to tell you to your face and not in a letter or on the telephone. I just didn't know it was going to be so *difficile*."

She paused.

"You like to think I have all the answers," she continued, "and sometimes I know I'm so full of myself to think that I do. I knew I had to tell you, but I didn't know how hard it was going to be. In the end, I made a mess of it . . . and I'm sorry in my heart about that."

I felt the urge to ask Phil if she loved me, even in the smallest way, but that would be one of my typical *manboy* questions, only thinking about myself. I didn't have any right asking that question anyway. I did have something that needed saying, even though I knew it would come out in my usual awkwardness.

"I won't be writing you as much, but it's not because I'm m-m-mad at you or anything," I said. "I finally realized that my writing was *for me* and not *to you*. I need to be m-m-more honest with myself about that."

It was true. I wasn't mad. I was hurt, but I wasn't mad. Phil had the courage to map out the path she knew was the best for us. I didn't have that courage yet. *Was I still a manboy?* All I knew is that I would be working on getting rid of that curse all by myself.

I grabbed Phil's hand and put it on the gearshift knob, my hand covering hers. I needed to show her I understood the finality of our situation.

"But you have to promise me you'll be careful in the N-N-Navy and in the helicopters if you go to Vietnam," I said. "I only know one swamp rabbit-chasing Cajun girl who . . . ."

Phil put her finger to my lips, lightly brushed my cheek with a kiss that felt more like a handshake and bounded from the car in a single motion with her helicopter bag over her shoulder. Her sore toe was no impediment to her fast escape from my car. She was inside the heavy double doors of Central Station and gone.

I had wondered if there might be a final kiss, how our final goodbye would play out, but as usual, Phil took care of it. I remained in the car without any last words to remember and only with the hollow feeling that her way might be the best for both of us.

I don't know how long I sat in the car. A loud whistle jarred me out of my stupor. I could hear the steel wheels grinding on the rails as I found myself walking through the station doors. The City of New Orleans was moving out. Each car jarred into motion as the couplers tightened and the force of the diesel engine overcame the inertia of each car one by one.

I stood on the concrete platform. A baggage handler hooked a line of empty carts together and pulled them toward the station. As he passed by, he asked: "Didn't miss your train, did you, son?"

The impromptu question only required the customary shake of my head, but unplanned words tumbled out of my mouth instead.

"Maybe I did . . . but that's another story." I smiled.

The baggage handler and his carts moved on toward the station. I eased off the concrete platform and put my leather-soled loafer on the rail. The vibrations were the same. Coming and going.

CHAPTER 15

THE FRATERNITY HOUSE was empty at 6:45 a.m.

In my tiny attic room, I folded my good newspaper clothes into my father's old piece of luggage he had given me. I stuffed my baseball glove and the remainder of my belongings into a duffel bag. The suitcase would fit in the passenger seat of my car and the duffel could be wedged in front of the seat on the floorboard. There would be room for the textbooks in my trunk that I would be able to sell back to the bookstore at a substantial loss but still with a little cash in hand.

In the chapter room, I wrote a note to the second-semester pledge who would be going through initiation soon, folded it and thumbtacked it to the bulletin board, writing "Jersey" on the outside.

> *Need to sell my pin that you like so much. Paid $350 for it. You can have it for $300. I'll call you tonight. – Vic.*

I was sure Jersey would bite on the good deal since he had told me he was going to get a pin just like mine when he went active. That $300 and the money for my books would see me through to find a room to rent in Memphis. The newspaper would be my home. Nellie's tumble-down shack in Coldwater, Mississippi, would be my home-away-from-home if I could make myself worthy of it.

Long-range planning usually brought on the worry-haints, but they didn't seem to be hovering around me as my plans progressed. I seemed to miss their company like a crump in my sock that had mysteriously disappeared.

With my suitcase in one hand and duffel bag over my shoulder, I headed out of the chapter room, wondering if this would be my last time to see the fraternity house that I had thought of as home but now felt a satisfaction in putting it behind me.

Robert E. Lee and his horse, Traveler, looked at me from the large painting that hung over the stone fireplace. I had never noticed the sadness in their eyes.

THE TODDLE HOUSE on Union Avenue was busy with the morning crowd that seemed to be getting back to normal. I had a few minutes to kill before my 8 a.m. shift. I ordered a cup of coffee.

"How you take that, honey?" the waitress asked.

"Black," I said, and then added, "As the b-b-bottom of a well." I knew I would stutter on the plosive sound of the B, but it felt like a proper way to ease my foot up off the brake.

I found a morning newspaper that had been left on a nearby table. Another three-line headline, but this one went just halfway across the front page:

More Troops Guard Capitol

As New Violence Rocks U.S.;

March To Attract Thousands

The story said Coretta Scott King, Dr. King's widow, was going to lead a march through downtown Memphis starting at 11 a.m. The police chief said he expected up to 30,000 marchers. A one-column headline at the bottom of the page caught my eye.

118 Enemy Killed

Near Khe Sanh

I chose not to read the Vietnam story and found myself turning the pages of the newspaper without the words registering.

With my glorious weekend of parties and celebrations shattered, feeling sorry for myself would have been about par for the course along with a visit from the worry-haints, but fresh thoughts swirled inside me. While I was not sure when or if I would get over Phil's plans that didn't include me, I could feel a new path emerging. A path that might be lonely, but at least it would be mine.

I pulled my reporter's notebook from my back pocket, found a fresh page and started playing around with the lead of a story. A pen was not as good as a typewriter, but I told myself it was the words that were important.

THE COPYDESK was just finishing up the Mid-South edition when I clocked in for my shift. I checked my mail slot for arrest reports to type but was surprised to find the slot empty. When I asked the city editor why there were no arrest records, without looking up from the galley proof he was reading, he said "talk to your buddy Chis."

My first thought was to take his sarcastic answer without comment, especially since it came from a newsroom superior, but I had just lost Phil and I was tired of being the one doing all the giving.

"What did you m-m-mean by that?" I asked. The city editor ignored me.

"If you have s-s-something to say to me, go ahead and say it," I said, making sure he was aware of my eyes drilling into him. The city editor waved me off with a flick of his hand. "I'm busy," he said. Phil was gone, but possibly she had left me a little of her backbone.

Chis was respected in the newsroom more than the city editor. As a lowly copy clerk, I had avoided workplace politics, but that would be changing.

I made my way over to Chis's desk where he was editing galley proofs. He peered at me over his reading glasses and smiled.

"We've had a breakthrough, Vic. No more arrest reports until we come up with a new policy on identifying race in crime stories," Chis said with an excitement that was unusual for him. "The editor appointed me to head up a newsroom committee to look into it."

Chis winked at me. "I think we may be finished with this race identification malarkey."

I smiled and turned away, but then pulled my foot completely off the brake.

"I like the word "m-m-malarkey," I said. "Did you know the word was coined by a newspaper cartoonist in Ireland?"

"No, I did not," Chis said. "Thanks for sharing that." Chis gave me a quizzical look. My comment had come out of nowhere, but I was proud of its spontaneity and that I could feel my internal brake losing its hold on me.

I went to the noisy wire room to pull copy. I had just witnessed a shift—Phil's father would have called it a sea change—a reversal of a long-established policy that I had never recognized as being racist but was exactly that. When you see something every day, it becomes part of the landscape, no matter if it's right or wrong. The status quo lets you escape from having to think for yourself. Start examining life on its face, I told myself. Look at the *prima facie* evidence, as the court reporters liked to call it, and not at someone else's interpretation. I thought how good it would be to share all of this with Phil in a long letter, but then I remembered I was on my own now, but I didn't feel my usual loneliness.

Did I let Phil go too easily? Did I give up without a fight for what I thought I so desperately wanted . . . needed? No. I did the right thing and the worry-haints were just going to have to live with it.

TWIST 'N SHOUT had drawn darkroom duties again for the day of the march. He caught up with me sorting the dozens of black-and-white photos that had piled up at the wire photo machine. He asked me if I had time to do a film pickup for the Final edition. Two photographers had been assigned to the downtown protest march, but the city desk had told them to stay with the crowd in case there might be violence. I should bring their film back and Twist 'n Shout would process the rolls.

"I'll be glad to get it," I said. "I'd like to see what's going on out there anyway. Seems like we're missing everything if we stay all closed up in here."

My new conversational tone was not lost on Twist 'n Shout. He gave me an odd look.

"Whatever tickles your pickle," he said.
I SQUEEZED the staff car into a small space at the Greyhound Bus Station loading dock just off Third Street. The spot was reserved for the newspaper clerks when picking up packages coming in from regional correspondents on the buses.

The photographers had informed the city desk on their hand-held radios that they were a half-block in front of the march leaders and that they would meet me at Main and Beale to hand off their rolls of film. I walked west on Union Avenue and saw the sea of marchers on Main Street. Most of the throng was Black, but I noticed a few whites in the mix and not just young people. For such a large gathering on a street that was flanked by tall concrete buildings, the crowd was eerily quiet as it marched.

I stepped into the street and found myself caught in the slow current of the people. A young man with a red and yellow armband designating him as a "Marshal Captain" cleared a spot for me in the throng. "Good to have you, Brother," he said. He called out his well-rehearsed orders. "Keep off the sidewalks. No smoking. No gum chewing. Join arms, brothers and sisters. Mine eyes have seen the glory."

 I marched with them. Never fight the current, Mr. Spiro had said. I didn't.

I understood at that moment what Nellie meant when she said that *we always are who we were.* There's no sense in trying to make excuses for the past. The only thing to do was to recognize what needed to be changed and start making the changes.

THE ALL-CAP HEADLINE in Monday's Final edition was a surprise when I pulled it off the press conveyor to take upstairs to the waiting editors.

U.S., HANOI AGREE TO TALKS

The all-cap play headline of the same size in the earlier Home edition had read:

THOUSANDS HONOR DR. KING

For some reason, the Vietnam War had replaced the peaceful downtown march as the top story in the paper on that Monday afternoon. I passed out the first copies of the Final edition to the editors in the newsroom.

"Even though everything was peaceful, shouldn't we have k-k-kept the play headline in the Final edition on Dr. King and the march," I said, when I handed Chis his paper. "Agreeing to talks doesn't mean much in V-V-Vietnam. Seems like they're always agreeing to something that doesn't mean anything."

I had never questioned the story placement or news judgment of anyone at the paper.

"Valid point, Vic," Chis said. "I felt like I had won enough battles for the day, so I didn't challenge the change in the Final." He winked at me. "Only good thing about it is that we get to do it all over again tomorrow . . . and we have yet another chance to get it right."

There was enough time to pull the copy off the state wires before my shift ended. A story on the Mississippi wire in a roundup of state briefs caught my eye.

> MOON LAKE, Miss. (UPI) – Two Coahoma County men sustained injuries late Saturday night in a skirmish at Conway's, a once-popular supper club on the shores of Moon Lake.
>
> The Coahoma County sheriff's department said one of the men received internal injuries after being kicked violently in the groin area. Another man reported being assaulted with a "medieval-style weapon of torture." Both were treated at a local hospital and released.

Witnesses were quoted as saying that the men were attacked without provocation by a young woman with a heavy foreign accent and her male accomplice. The two escaped in a small convertible of undetermined make.

Anyone having any information should contact the Coahoma County sheriff's department.

I smiled. I wasn't Philomene Moreau's boyfriend, a role I had so desperately coveted, but I was proud to be her "accomplice." I could understand how my coffee-cup holder with its lead base and coat-hanger spikes might be confused as a "medieval-style weapon of torture." I would tell my buddy in the newspaper's stereotype department that I had misplaced mine and would ask him to make me another one of his handy gadgets for my car.

That wire story and hundreds more like it would go on a copydesk spike for the next news cycle and eventually into a waste can.

With my shift over and the newsroom clearing out for the day, I sat down at the typewriter that I considered the best one on the city desk. The police radio that was never turned off cackled on about more white Mustangs being stopped in the area even though Dr. King had been assassinated four days before and the perpetrator surely had left the Memphis by now. I threaded paper and carbon into the typewriter and pulled out my notebook from my back pocket. I typed.

The cover of the book is green, but that's not where it gets its name.

Victor Hugo Green, a New York City postal worker who died in 1960, is the founder of the "Green Book," an underground guide that informs Black travelers in the U.S. where they can eat and spend the night without fear of discrimination.

I needed a direct quote from Walter Bailey, the owner of the Lorraine Motel. I looked up the motel's number in the telephone book. A voice that I recognized answered.

"Lorraine Motel."

"This is V-V-Vic Vollmer of the Pr-Pr-Press-Scimitar," I said. "Could I speak with Mr. Walter Bailey."

"Yeah, I 'member talkin' to you a couple days ago," the voice said. "Uh, Mr. Bailey ain't here. He's still at the hospital with Mrs. Bailey. They ain't sure she's gonna make it."

"Oh, sorry to hear that," I said. "I was wondering if you m-m-might answer a few questions about that Green Book."

"Don't know nothing about it, like I told you, and I ain't supposed to be talking to no one about nothing," the desk clerk said.

"Well, could I have your n-n-name for my story. I need . . . ." The line went dead.

I would have to get my direct quotes and information from a call to the New York offices of *The Green Book*. The worry-haints would be my combatants on the long-distance call, but I knew the best way to deal with them now was by concentrating on the search for the right words to put down on paper in just the right way. The way that Dr. King used words when he spoke.

I jumped up and ran to my drawer at the copy clerks' worktable. Dr. King's speech transcribed by the wires was where I left it. I took off the rubber band and let the long sheet of wire copy unfurl.

When I had first read the speech as it came off the wire machine, I was confused by Dr. King's relating of his journey through time beginning in Egypt and the Red Sea. Then Plato, Aristotle, Socrates. Then the emperors of the Roman Empire. On to the Renaissance and his namesake Martin Luther. Abraham Lincoln after that and then President Roosevelt's "nothing to fear but fear itself." He had summed up the whole of human history in a few sentences.

Nellie's words—*we always are who we were*—came back to me in their full measure. She wasn't talking about just me. Or even all the people in my small world. She was talking about all of humankind, just like Dr. King. Even when Nellie said it, the phrase seemed incomplete. Something was missing.

We always are who we were . . . but the past does not own the future.

I had just lost Phil, but a solace came over me that I was exactly where I needed to be. Phil had to have helicopters to take her where she wanted to go. I would maneuver on my journey with words on paper.

The answer for me was not to go dead inside. I had a lot of writing to look forward to and that was making me feel alive.

From the Author

Manboy, as with the other two books of the trilogy—*Paperboy* and *Copyboy*—is a purposeful blend of eye-witnessed events and fiction; a curious amalgam of "I-was-there" and imagination; a circuitous space inhabited by both real and imaginary people.

Indeed, my storytelling is so intertwined with these variables that when discussing my books, I find myself having to pause and think carefully about the decade (1959-1968) of my life if I am to separate fact from fiction.

One event, however, that will be forever etched in my non-fiction consciousness took place on a weekday afternoon in March 1994.

As managing editor of *The Knoxville News-Sentinel*, I was a member of a Leadership Knoxville class that visited the Riverbend Maximum Security Institution in Nashville, a branch of the Tennessee state prison system. The facility, supposedly a showcase in the field of incarceration, had only been open a few years. Our group arrived by bus for an afternoon tour to see first-hand how a modern penal facility operated.

As with most prisons, the various buildings contained a complicated labyrinth of long halls and iron bars. Our class of around thirty members had split up into smaller groups led by different correctional officers. Unlike maximum-security prisons depicted in movies, the modern facility we were being led through was immaculate and quiet. No slamming gates. No horns. No buzzers. No conversations.

My small group had gotten ahead of me. At the next corner in the hall, I turned the wrong way. Ten feet in front of me was a double row of iron bars blocking off the hall. A corrections officer flipped through his work papers at his standing desk behind the first set of bars. A man in standard prison clothing leaned on a floor mop behind the second row of bars. He looked at me with black and hollow eyes.

The eyes of James Earl Ray.

I had grown up in Memphis and worked at newspapers there for the first 15 years of my career. I had followed closely the worldwide manhunt for Ray, his capture and trial. I had coordinated with journalists who covered his 1977 escape from Brushy Mountain State Penitentiary in East Tennessee and his recapture three days later. Over the years, I had thumbed through many dozens of photos of the convicted assassin, choosing ones for publication in newspapers where I worked.

Those eyes and my imagination quickly carried me back 26 years to Memphis.

On April 4, 1968, a rifle barrel poked out of a rear window of a down-trodden rooming house on South Main. The murderous eyes of James Earl Ray sighted down the barrel of the hunting rifle at a target, 203 feet away, at the Lorraine Motel. In my mind I could hear the rifle's report; saw Dr. Martin Luther King slump to the ground; heard his last breaths call for the gospel song: "Take My Hand, Precious Lord."

History tells us that James Earl Ray was born into poverty in Missouri and was a petty criminal from an early age. He spent his early life in and out of prisons. He lived under many aliases and was an avowed racist and Nazi sympathizer. Ray's white Mustang was found abandoned in an Atlanta parking lot on April 11, 1968. Ray was arrested in London by Scotland Yard on June 8, 1968, after a worldwide manhunt. He was returned to Memphis and eventually pled guilty to the assassination of Dr. Martin Luther King on March 10, 1969, Ray's 41st birthday. He was sentenced to life in prison, escaping the death penalty in exchange for his guilty plea.

For the record, Loree Bailey, wife of Walter Bailey and co-owner of the Lorraine Motel and for whom the motel was named, died on April 9, 1968, the same day as Dr. King's funeral in Atlanta attended by more than 100,000 people. Mrs. Bailey suffered a stroke when she heard the fatal shot fired and never recovered. Walter Bailey continued to operate the facility but would never again rent out Room 306. The motel area is now the site of the National Civil Rights Museum.

I stiffened as the lone inmate and I stared at each other, probably no more than ten seconds, but for what now seems like an eternity. The grey-haired prisoner eventually dipped his mop into a bucket on wheels, turned and pushed down the hall in the ambling gait of a weary man.

Several others in my group also had caught unexpected glimpses of Ray during the tour. We nervously chatted about the assassin as we boarded the bus for the ride back to Knoxville. We all agreed that we would never forget looking into those heinous eyes.

Legions of conspiracy theorists in the past fifty years have tried to connect the assassination to different fringe groups and their ill-conceived causes. The only conspiracy was that between a psychopath and his racist mentality, or as Dr. King alluded to in his final speech on April 3, 1968, one of "our sick white brothers."

James Earl Ray, age 70, died in Riverbend prison on April 23, 1998—30 years and 19 days after he murdered Dr. Martin Luther King.

A Note About the Boy Trilogy

During the past 10 years, I've been privileged to speak at hundreds of schools about my writing. Knowing that much of my fiction is autobiographical, I'm frequently asked how I manage to recall events of my youth—I'm 77 now—in such detail. My answers have been fuzzy, but I'm beginning to understand the proper response.

For young people who stutter, the condition is confusing and traumatic. Stuttering events become seared in the consciousness under the labels of embarrassment, shame and inadequacy. We simply don't have the maturity to know better. An inner voice continues the adolescent scream: "What's wrong with me?"

In the quest for that answer, our young minds put our thoughts and feelings under an uncompromising microscope, which only begins to achieve a focus with age and maturity. The emotional scars may become less noticeable, but they remain scars.

The careful reader of the trilogy will recognize that the first-person "voice" of the protagonist is different at the three stages of his life. Indeed, I have come to feel that my 11-year-old self is responsible for *Paperboy*; the 17-year-old version of me wrote *Copyboy*; the 21-year-old me wrote *Manboy*. I emerge from a writing session with the mindful surprise of arthritic knees and the shuffling gait of an old man.

"Would you have written your stories if you weren't a person who stuttered?" asks a young student. I give a long and convoluted response. The simple answer is "no."

"But you're glad you wrote them, aren't you?"

Yes.

Vince Vawter
September 2023